Mama, I See You

Mama, I See You

Finding Glimmers of Hope
in the Trenches of Motherhood

Mirette Abraham

Illustrations by Maria Hakim

RESOURCE *Publications* · Eugene, Oregon

MAMA, I SEE YOU
Finding Glimmers of Hope in the Trenches of Motherhood

Resource Publications
An Imprint of Wipf and Stock Publishers
199 W. 8th Ave., Suite 3
Eugene, OR 97401

www.wipfandstock.com

PAPERBACK ISBN: 978-1-6667-3633-5
HARDCOVER ISBN: 978-1-6667-9447-2
EBOOK ISBN: 978-1-6667-9448-9

JANUARY 10, 2022 2:55 PM

Contents

Acknowledgments

THIS BOOK IS DEDICATED to my loving husband, R. You are the reason I strive to be a better mother. With your patience and unconditional love in your fatherhood, you show me how Christ loves each one of us. I want to emulate that love, and I am reminded how to do so each day living with you because of your perfect example.

To my baby, L. Your pure love and exciting energy are so inspiring and truly a reflection of how intricately and perfectly God fashions each of us. I am blessed beyond measure in being your mama, and I can't wait to see how you end up changing the world.

To my baby, G. You blessed us when things felt darker than they had ever been. You are the streak of hope we were so desperately praying for, and when you finally join us, you will see just how loved you are.

To my mama, A. Your strength, resilience, and complete faith are admirable. You've set the standard for me. Because of your nurturing wisdom I have a constant image of faithful motherhood in you.

Finally, to all the mothers out there, trying hard to leave their mark in this world. We strive to set the perfect footprint in the sand, wishing that the waves will never wash it away. But what we need to do is make this life become a seal of love in the hearts of everyone we meet, allowing our choices and experiences to hum a melody of gratitude to our Maker.

Author's Note

I'VE WRITTEN THIS BOOK hoping to unveil everything that keeps us from fulfilling the perfect life that our Lord has in store for us and to encourage us all to reflect on how He uses everything and everyone in our path to make that mystery known. Throughout the chapters, I share my personal journey of reflection and bring to light my Lord's love and grace in my motherhood—both the struggles He allows and the flowers that bloom in the wreckage.

Introduction

Start by doing what's necessary; then do what's possible;
and suddenly you are doing the impossible.

—ST FRANCIS OF ASSISI

I'M CONSTANTLY PLAGUED BY the thought that I am not fulfilling my purpose, that I'm not living out the life God set out for me.

Am I doing enough?

Am I being enough?

Am I enough?

But enough for what and who? Am I really trying to be enough for God, or am I trying to live this 'perfect' life that the world tells me is the only way to live?

What am I even pursuing?

The lines blur between the surreal perfection of life and my reality. I get stuck daydreaming about what I 'should' do based on society's standards and how to marry that with what the Lord is asking of me.

That day, the one during the week I turned thirty, I walked down the corridor with my tail between my legs and an inaudible moping that was palpable in my mere presence. I was sad. But I was the petty kind of sad. There was no joy in aging. I'd always tried to live a life of significance, when every decision and every path taken would lead to something important. I placed weight on even the smallest decisions and put the greatest pressure on the simplest of plans. It was fine to have some fun, encouraged even, but it couldn't be with just anyone. In fact, the company I kept always had to better me. Basically, I wanted to change the world, and growing up just meant less time to do so. I was thirty, and my world did not differ from the year before.

Just as my thoughts were getting ready to run their hundredth lap, a colleague interrupted the train, asking about a patient. She must've noticed my sullenness because she asked me if I was okay.

I was okay.

I just expected the world to be a better place by now.

I mean, how many people had turned to Christ because of me in my thirty years on this earth?

How many people wake up each day knowing that they are truly loved because of me?

How many of my friends believed that our friendship was leading us both to the Kingdom, rather than just allowing us to pass the little time we had?

I was thirty and felt as though I had no treasure built up in heaven.

But I knew I was okay. We were in the middle of a pandemic after all (more on that later), and this was the furthest thing from a valid complaint! So, I simply mustered a melancholic, "I'm just moping because I'm aging. I turn thirty this week."

I was met with bafflement. She couldn't understand my lack of excitement about my birthday.

I defended my stance, "I am excited about my birthday; I mean, I make my family celebrate me for an entire month! The part I don't like is growing up. Ironic, I know."

"Why does growing up upset you?" She asked, "Are you not proud of everything you've achieved to date?"

Her questions initially confused me, and then I remembered she hadn't been audience to my preceding thoughts. She couldn't understand my drive for significance, and I didn't really feel like getting into a long discussion in which I would have to answer questions pertaining to my character and faith. I wasn't ready for that kind of scrutiny yet.

She must have realized I didn't know how to answer her question, so she halted my bewilderment with a simpler question, "You're turning thirty and you have a loving husband, a gorgeous daughter, a house, an income, a fulfilling job, and a killer personality. Which of those things are you upset about?"

The truth is, I was proud of all those things, and her question pierced my soul, reminding me that I needed to be grateful. But it's not that easy, and the reason for my discontent went far deeper than our superficial conversation. What followed her question was not gratitude on my part, but, sadly, guilt. It added to the bindle of guilt I had already been lugging around for a few years.

I was in no place for gratitude. I had barely made it to a place of acceptance.

Instragram-able

Perfectly Imperfect - We have all heard that no two snowflakes are alike. Each snowflake takes the perfect form for the maximum efficiency and effectiveness for its journey. And while the universal force of gravity gives them a shared destination, the expansive pace in the air gives each snowflake the opportunity to take their own path. They are on the same journey, but each takes a different path.

Along this gravity-driven journey, some snowflakes collide and damage each other, some collide and join together, some are influenced by wind... there are so many transitions and changes that take place along the journey of the snowflake. But, no matter what the transition, the snowflake always finds itself perfectly shaped for its journey.

I find parallels in nature to be a beautiful reflection of grand orchestration. One of these parallels is of snowflakes and us. We, too, are all headed in the same direction. We are being driven by a universal force to the same destination. We are all individuals taking different journeys and along our journey, we sometimes bump into each other, we cross paths, we become altered... we take different physical forms. But at all times we too are 100% perfectly imperfect. At every given moment we are absolutely perfect for what is required for our journey. I'm not perfect for your journey and you're not perfect for my journey, but I'm perfect for my journey and you're perfect for your journey. We're heading to the same place, we're taking different routes, but we're both exactly perfect the way we are.

Think of what understanding this great orchestration could mean for relationships. Imagine interacting with others knowing that they too each share this parallel with the snowflake. Like you, they are headed to the same place and no matter what they may appear like to you, they have taken the perfect form for their journey. How strong our relationships would be if we could see and respect that we are all perfectly imperfect for our journey."

— Steve Maraboli, Life, the Truth, and Being Free

Chapter 1

Instagram-able

We have all heard that no two snowflakes are alike. Each snowflake takes the perfect form for the maximum efficiency and effectiveness for its journey. And while the universal force of gravity gives them a shared destination, the expansive space in the air gives each snowflake the opportunity to take their own path. They are on the same journey, but each takes a different path.

Along this gravity-driven journey, some snowflakes collide and damage each other, some collide and join together, some are influenced by wind . . . there are so many transitions and changes that take place along the journey of the snowflake. But, no matter what the transition, the snowflake always finds itself perfectly shaped for its journey. I find parallels in nature to be a beautiful reflection of grand orchestration. One of these parallels is of snowflakes and us. We, too, are all headed in the same direction. We are being driven by a universal force to the same destination. We are all individuals taking different journeys and along our journey, we sometimes bump into each other, we cross paths, we become altered . . . we take different physical forms. But at all times we too are 100% perfectly imperfect. At every given moment we are absolutely perfect for what is required for our journey. I'm not perfect for your journey and you're not perfect for my journey, but I'm perfect for my journey and you're perfect for your journey. We're heading to the same place, we're taking different routes, but we're both exactly perfect the way we are.

Think of what understanding this great orchestration could mean for relationships. Imagine interacting with others knowing that they too each share this parallel with the snowflake. Like you, they are headed to the same place and no matter what they may appear like to you, they have taken the perfect form for their journey. How strong our relationships would be if we could see and respect that we are all perfectly imperfect for our journey.

— STEVE MARABOLI,
LIFE, THE TRUTH, AND BEING FREE

THE OTHER DAY I READ a caption on social media that pulled at my gut a little. I don't really think that's a common phrase, or that something can actually 'pull' at one's gut, but that's what it did. The caption made me feel a little ill and anxious, all while sparking a train of thought that led to an anger that sat right in my core.

And I didn't know why.

Someone posted a gorgeous photo of their family—the couple and their two young children—and ended the caption with this sentence: "Our life isn't Instagram-able right now." I don't remember the rest because that's the part that pulled at my gut.

What is "Instagram-able?"

Why have we set such ridiculous expectations for what we can and can't post on the internet? Worse, why have we applied these standards to our lives? What makes my life less "Instagramable" than yours?

"In the world you will have tribulation . . ." ~ John 16:33

That's one thing we can be sure of in our lives: tribulation. God didn't promise clarity, but He guaranteed stained glass windows—at some parts, you just can't see through, but when you put all the pieces together, you get a beautiful, imperfect piece of art that reflects its unique light on everything it touches.

That's us.

That's how we need to see ourselves and our lives—every aspect, the Instagram-able and the not-so-Instagram-able. They all come together to create our Lord's masterpiece, and the good can't exist without the bad. Actually, I don't think we can even appreciate or acknowledge the good without first experiencing the bad.

Our measure of 'good' isn't accurate anyway. We forever chase the unattainable, sacrificing precious fleeting moments in this life searching for the nonexistent. We convince ourselves that the stained glass needs to look a certain way, even though all the pieces fit in perfect unison with each other, allowing His creation to take shape. With each gust of wind, or clumsy glassmaker, the pieces are picked back up and placed in their spots to finish the job and present to the Master the entire purpose for their very creation.

If my measure of what's 'good' is subjective and skewed toward the emotional attachments I have formed with the experiences I have had, then I'm the one who ultimately decides what is deemed "Instagram-able."

Along the lines of our inaccurate measure of what is 'good', the question of God's 'goodness' comes up often, especially when someone is already questioning their faith or looking for reasons to cut off ties with God.

"Why do *bad* things happen to *good* people?"

Every single one of us has asked this question. And every single one of us has searched for a simple answer to it.

We want to know why a kid died of a horrific and painful illness with so much love to live for.

We want to know why a single woman was raped and killed, leaving behind her toddler and newborn.

We want to know why the sweet old lady was attacked by an intruder and left for dead in her own home.

We want to know why the young must flee the war in their countries, seeking refuge in a tiny boat on the raging and unpredictable sea.

We want to know why, even though we go to church, pray fervently, love our neighbor, give our tithes, and respect our elders, we lost our job, and just can't make ends meet, no matter how long and hard we fast!

We want answers to a standard that we have limited God to.

We want the exact measurements for things confined to a metric system that changes its parameters with each new experience, emotion, and outcome.

Having a two-year-old has given me the slightest glimpse into what I think God hears when we continue to question His goodness, His sovereignty. My daughter and I were experimenting with crafts one Sunday afternoon for virtual Sunday School (as I briefly mentioned, we were in the middle of a pandemic, but more on that later) when she asked to cut her own shapes out of the paper we were using. I handed her the plastic scissors that my mom had bought for her. She cried and fussed, asking to use the scissors that were in my hand. I showed her the sharp edges and pointy tips, running her little finger across them so she could appreciate what I was trying to explain. She nodded, but still asked, "How about only once?" still not grasping how dangerous this little tool can be. I said "no" again and explained once more why she couldn't have them. She cried and yelled, throwing her own scissors on the floor. After a minute, she picked herself up, looked at me, and said, "Mommy, you're not my best friend anymore."

As juvenile as this encounter was, that line broke me.

I felt as though I had failed her; I failed to make her see what I see and appreciate the love and care in my simple "no."

What she saw and heard did not align with her emotions. My "no" did not fit into her box of desires, no matter how 'good' it really was. She could only identify my 'goodness' as 'badness' through her young, emotionally tainted lens.

Sound familiar?

Recently my husband was made redundant from a job that was so good for us. It paid our phone bills and health insurance; he had a great salary working only four days a week, and for most (if not all) of those days he could work from home, which meant he was doing all the heavy lifting when it came to tending to the house and looking after our daughter. It allowed me to go to work, spending hours longer than I should looking after people I'll never meet again, with a little less guilt weighing me down. It seemed like a dream. Then, suddenly, it was gone. It was for no real reason other than the company wasn't doing as well as they'd hoped and they needed to let go of their most recent hires, which unfortunately included my husband.

We were fine. But part of me felt sadness. This wasn't the first time life threw us into a pit of uncertainty and fear, anxious about what would follow, not knowing how long the financial burden would continue beating us down. When we were first married, I was still a medical student, and he had quite a low-paying job. We were literally living paycheck to paycheck, struggling to make rent and fearing how much longer we would be inconveniencing our parents. My husband went through a period of self-revelation, realizing that he wasn't fulfilling his ultimate life's purpose by carrying on in his current role. He searched and prayed and finally found his foot-in-the-door job that would eventually get him where he wanted to be. But then that ended abruptly, without explanation and without a fallback. We were young and both unemployed, without a single source of income for our simple lives. But we trusted and prayed, even through the hurt, and sure enough, God came through.

There's never doubt about His grace, given to us undeservingly daily. Regardless of how often we turn our backs on Him, He continues to be true and merciful. We never know when or how He'll come through for us. Sometimes we wonder if He wants us to go through the storm entirely alone to come out the other end unafraid of the lightning. We're constantly searching for explanations for why He would let us endure something that we think is an easy fix for Him.

Why couldn't my husband just keep his job? What effort would it take from the All Knowing to prevent the conversation with his manager? We obviously weren't greedy with money and already appreciated its value, so why did it have to be taken away? We tried to find a rational explanation for what happened.

But how can logic explain the Indefinite?

When has our understanding ever been able to capture the Unlimited?

How can you appreciate the entire ocean when you've only ever seen water held in a glass?

When my husband lost his job this second time, there was a wave of certainty in the air. I was certain that this was for the best. I knew in my heart that God was taking away our tiny little jewel to give us an entire box of valuables. Better was coming. I didn't know what or when or even how—but it was coming.

Today, we have money coming into our bank account that is completely unaccounted for. I can't explain it. Logic can't explain it. But it's happening.

Today, we are both doing what we love and are ever so grateful for the journey and the lessons we learned along the way.

Today, we know we are held by the very hand that fashioned the stars in the night sky and orchestrates the movements of the planets and moon.

He's got this.

He's got us.

But these are not the things that people know about us or that brings us 'likes' on our social media feeds. We don't share our insecurities and our pains for fear of appearing vulnerable and broken. Perfection is an ideology we have created over the years based on unattainable goals, and we've established that we base our idea of perfection on our emotional attachments to certain experiences. So, what is the emotional attachment to brokenness and vulnerability? Why is it so important for me to conceal the realities of what makes me who I am?

In the face of uncertainty, when we have absolutely no ability to stand on our own knowledge nor any foresight of how a situation will unfold, do we turn to God for answers? Or, in pursuing this mythical perfection, have we lost sight of who we are and who our Lord is?

The reality is that we are broken, and, because of that, we feel vulnerable. So why is it so important for others to see something other than the truth?

Ultimately, the answer lies in what we value most.

To know where our values lie, though, we need to break it down even more and rediscover the reasons for our existence.

We must ask, "Why was I created? And why am I here?"

The answer to the first question is simple: love. I was created as a result of my Lord's pure love. Why He loves me, though, is a question I'll never know the answer to.

Now, the answer to why I am here is not that simple. People spend their entire lives searching for that answer, trying to find where they fit in this world and what difference they can make. We all want to live for significance, but sadly, most of us end up living for survival or even success. We live day-to-day, either trying to make it to the next day or trying to make it up the ranks. But where is the significance in either of those approaches?

I know that most of my days parenting are lived with the sole aim of surviving. I struggle through the opinions and tantrums, convincing myself that if I can only make it to bedtime, I'll be okay. I don't end up savoring the purity and joy in my daughter's youngest years because I'm continually praying them away.

So how do we live for significance?

We can answer that by answering why we are here, the reason for our existence. Even more simply put, the answer lies with our Maker. If I want to know why I was created, I need to ask my Creator. He designed me intricately and for a very specific reason. Instead of running to Him for answers, though, I look elsewhere, hoping that eventually I will find what I'm looking for. The more time we spend with our Maker, the more time He has to mold us into His ultimate warrior and finally start using us as He intended. The closer we get to Him, the more we become like Him and align our will with His. He perfects us. Yes, perfects us. Not the idealistic perfection we have been chasing for so long, but perfect imperfection that allows His glory to be revealed in our shortcomings and weaknesses.

Once I accept that I will find my purpose in the presence of my Savior, everything I do will align with His ultimate purpose for my life. My values will come from that very purpose, and I will no longer be so occupied with the world's perception of me and my choices. My focus will constantly be on God and how He sees me.

So, back to my first question: What is Instagram-able, anyway? The answer: Who cares?

Because we are all works in progress, being perfected daily by our Lord, our brokenness, flaws, and vulnerabilities only serve to bring Him glory, as He uses those exact things for His bigger purpose.

So, Mama, let's put ourselves at the feet of Christ and allow Him to fashion our motherhood for significance so that our lives can glorify He who loves us perfectly.

Now look up!

Father,

I pray we come to know You who loves our imperfections so perfectly.

I pray we come to see our worth through Your eyes and we can learn how You can use us in our weaknesses to bring glory to Your mighty name.

I pray we can see that our worth comes from knowing who we are in You. We are Your children, and You loved me enough to spread out Your undefiled hands on the cross and die for me.

I pray we realize we, like the stars, were deliberately created, made with specific intent for a particular purpose, and that purpose will be revealed through the very insecurities we are running away from.

I pray we become so overwhelmed by Your love that we realize we no longer need to come up for a breath of what this world is serving and come to find that You are enough. Even if I feel like I don't measure up, I know that You have used the most "un-Instagram-able" figures in history to do Your finest work.

Time to reflect . . .

1. What insecurities do you feel are holding you back from discovering your worth?

2. What do you feel your values are right now, and how might this change if you surrender your will to His?

3. Do you believe God can use your insecurities for good? Why or why not?

4. What practical steps can you take to discover your ultimate purpose? (Hint: Goals need to be SMART—specific, measurable, attainable, relevant, and timely.)

Mom-guilt

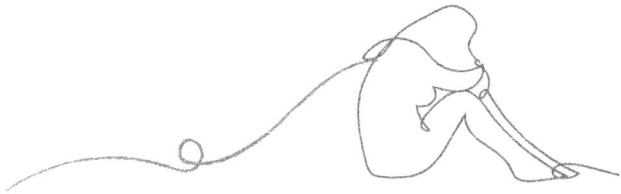

"*P*arenting and working is one of the
biggest conflicts I've ever experienced.
Every bit of me wants to be with you
but doesn't want to lose me in the process.
I want you to know that it was for something.
I don't want "it all" but this is my something
while you are my everything."

— @mother_pukka

(Anna Whitehouse - Journalist and
Author of "Where's My Happy Ending?"

Chapter 2

Mom Guilt

Parenting and working is one of the biggest conflicts I've ever experienced. Every bit of me wants to be with you but doesn't want to lose me in the process.

I want you to know that it was for something.

I don't want "it all" but this is my something while you are my everything.

—ANNA WHITEHOUSE

EVERY DAY I FEEL GUILTY.

Guilty that I'm not there for my daughter while I work.

Guilty that I can't take her to all the activities her friends take part in during the workweek.

Guilty that she's learned wake-up time means I have to leave her.

"Know that you are my everything, and this is just something I have to do while I'm here. One day, baby, you'll know," I whisper to her as I hug her close before leaving. I hear the cracks forming deep in my soul—cracks that will fill with guilt, regret, and sadness as my day goes on, forming a solid knot of anxiety that sets up camp in my chest. It's a knot that never goes away; it only increases in size and weight. As moms, we give that heaviness a name and

15

let it live in our most sacred places. We provide it with its very own dwelling place, all set up with the finest décor, and we wait for the day it picks itself up and tells us it has found a better place to live. But it'll never leave as long as we are making it comfortable. We need to nudge it out of our lives without allowing that very action to fuel its growth. We need to fill our lives with so much love, joy, and positivity that it feels suffocated enough to pick itself up and walk out. And we need to fill our space with so much God that it no longer lords its supremacy over us.

He is the only one who can fix this.

He is the only one who can give us the freedom we thirst for.

He is the only one who can take this away and replace it with love. So much love. Only love.

> "Come to Me, all you who labor and are heavy laden, and I will give you rest . . . I am gentle and lowly in heart, and you will find rest for your souls. For My yoke is easy and My burden is light." ~ Matthew 11:28–29

That's what I want: someone to hold me close, to tell me it's all going to be okay, and to mean it. I want to feel as though the struggles and thoughts that I deem ridiculous are being heard as genuine problems, not just exaggerated nonsense on its way to being swept under the rug. I want to feel unconditional, nonjudgmental, true love that immerses me in its depth and consumes me completely, so the chatter surrounding me no longer has any effect.

I never talk about this next part. I've always tried to bury it deep in my little box of unknowns, denying that this was truly the case and constantly making excuses for myself. But writing about it is more cathartic than I thought. Please bear with me while I try to put all of this into words.

The time period following the birth of my daughter was the toughest period of my life.

Until recently, I was still picking up the few stragglers from the pieces of my life that covered the entire floor for months.

It was like I had stepped out of my skin for months and was trying to crawl back inside and claim my body again. The constant search for 'me' in this unfamiliar terrain felt like an impossible task. I was trying to tread water, but with every stroke, it seemed like more would come through my cracks and envelop me further. The more I tried, the deeper I went under. When I could finally come up for air, and it seemed my surroundings had eased a bit, I couldn't hear anything but a ringing or see anything but a thick fog, making everything hard to comprehend. Then the waters would swell again, pushing me farther and farther away from my destination—myself. The more I tried, the more fatigued I would get; the more I swam, the more I drowned; and the more I persevered, the harder the pushback.

The worst part was that God was letting this happen to me. He was watching as I cried out from the middle of the ocean and didn't send help. He heard me say to Him over and over that this was enough and I couldn't take anymore, but not a word. Then He heard me say, "I'm done treading, the waters can take me," and still nothing.

I was mad.

How could He let me go through this?

How could He sit in silence while His beloved was being torn to pieces by wolves?

Did He even care?

The punches kept rolling. That first year of my daughter's life, we had to move in with my parents for financial reasons, hoping to save enough money for a bigger house to accommodate our growing family. After that came months of rejection from employers for both my husband and I, even though our only reason for applying to those jobs was to make more time for each other and to serve Him.

To give you a bit of background, when I started medical school, I had my eyes and heart set on a career in oncology.[1] I had researched, arranged voluntary placements at certain centers, and decided quite early on that this is what I wanted to do. Cancer has always been a part of my life. I have lost countless relatives to it

---

1. The study of cancer and the practice of looking after those afflicted with cancer.

and have witnessed firsthand the effect of it on the lives of those I love—the pain, the sadness, the loneliness.

I was seventeen when I sat beside my dying grandmother in the ICU as she took some of her final assisted breaths, writhed in pain, and fought in confusion. I was there when her room filled with incense and the smell of roses while she settled back down and closed her eyes. I was there holding my mother's hand as they put her body in the ground, trying to stop my mother from throwing her own body in the ground where her loved one rested.

I was there when my twenty-six-year-old cousin was diagnosed with metastatic cancer,[2] having only recently given birth to twin baby girls and only being married for a short period. I was there when she sat beside us crying out in pain and asking Him to intervene. And I was there when we laid her to rest.

I saw the pain and felt the hurt many times, enough to know that I wouldn't want to be anywhere else. I wanted to be there to help ease the pain, or provide comfort where I could, for those who might not see many more days. The thought of death made me pray. It reminded me of my Lord's suffering and how much He sacrificed for us, and it made me want to be better for His children. Exposure to death made me realize just how fleeting and fragile this world really is. Nobody is immune to its cruelty. It made me look to heaven—and want it.

However, this life plan of mine became twisted and took a few turns, as they do, as I began my career. I completed a few geriatric[3] rotations in my early years and discovered my love for the elderly. I thought maybe this specialty was my calling and I could combine it with palliative care,[4] still fulfilling my desire for caring for the terminally ill. My boss at the time thought I was a good fit for the job and made it seem like all I had to do was pass

2. Cancer that has spread to other organs in the body, changing a person's management to only focusing on controlling their symptoms rather than prolonging survival.

3. Study of aged care and the practice of caring for the elderly.

4. A medical speciality and caregiving approach aimed at improving quality of life and alleviating suffering of patients with chronic or terminal illness.

my exams and he would have a job waiting for me. I liked that assurance (although, if you're in the medical field, you learn never to take someone's "word for it") and I liked that I no longer had to think about how or what I was going to apply for in the coming years. I completed my preliminary assessments for my first year of physician's training,[5] went through the hospital interviews, and got through it. I had a job lined up to begin my journey toward becoming a geriatrician. But I got cold feet. I pulled out. I still don't know the exact reason why I acted so rashly. Maybe I wanted kids and I thought the road ahead did not include that as an option, or maybe I was looking for an excuse to leave something I never truly wanted. Regardless, I didn't feel relieved—and I didn't know where I was heading.

Just as I was starting to regret my decision to pull out, I received an email asking if I wanted to apply for general practice the following year. The email came late in the year while the college usually runs their intake in April, so already that was fairly unusual. They were advertising a second round of applications since they had a few unfilled training spots they were hoping to fill within the next month. Only eight of those spots were remotely close to home. And even those weren't really close, but without young kids, it would be quite easy to travel to and from work each day. I prayed hard and eventually thought that maybe this was a sign to apply. Having this job meant I could have a child and I would never have to give up my church service; I could put God and my family at the forefront. I figured this exam could be my practice run, and if I did well, I could apply the following year and work closer to home. To my surprise, I did really well on the exam and naively thought that it was decided: I would become a general practitioner in Sydney, start my family, and never have to do another night shift again! So, I left the hospital, got pregnant, and signed up to take the entrance exam.

---

5. The pathway you take to become a medical specialist. Basically, it includes two years of general medical rotations, followed by the worst exams of your life, and then three years in the medical speciality of choice (for me, that would have been geriatrics).

But God allowed for yet another detour.

I failed the exam.

I failed hard!

"What? Why, Lord?"

I thought I was doing the 'noble' thing by applying for this job. I thought I was putting God and my family first, rather than my work, and I believed that was favorable in His sight.

I was working several temporary roles, so I was getting a fair bit of significant experience while having the flexibility to choose the days and shifts I worked. I was pregnant and tired all the time, so I didn't totally hate the thought of continuing in those roles for a bit longer.

"It's fine, I'll try again next year!"

But the next year I was different. I wasn't me. I didn't really know who I was, and I didn't know how to get 'me' back.

I applied, took the exam, and failed again—even worse than the last time.

Cue the confusion.

"Lord, don't You want this for me? Don't You want me to be happy? I'm telling You I want this thing that I strongly feel will allow me to have a family, be near them throughout my entire career, and have more time to serve You! Why don't You want the same? Why can't You give me this one tiny little thing that would literally take no effort from You? Aren't I suffering enough in this pit that You've left me in? When are you coming? Are You even coming?"

I spiraled further. I couldn't understand what was happening, and I just wanted some peace.

In addition to all this, after giving birth I suffered from pain that a myriad of investigations and specialists could not explain. I had to go through more surgery and hospital admissions to understand it. The months that followed my second failed exam included three admissions to the hospital, three specialist reviews, and more tests and medications than I could count. I didn't go a day without being hunched over in pain. I couldn't last a night without waking up and wishing for the pain to be taken away. Pain has this funny way of making everything around you louder. It heightens the screams of fear and sharpens the stabs of anxiety. Worse, it pushes you further into despair's embrace.

Through all this, my daughter was my emerging rainbow. My emerging rainbow didn't like to sleep though. The sleeplessness mingled with my constant pain, both holding me captive. They met the sorrow that was living in my heart, and together they claimed me. They wrapped themselves around my eyes and ankles, making it harder for me to continue to tread and impossible to see where I was heading. I was getting fatigued, and I was letting the waters take me under. I desperately wanted to give up. I spent all my car rides and showers in tears. My insides were being wrung out trying to rid themselves of the overflow of water that had made its way in. My hurt had completely claimed my identity. I didn't want anyone else to see my pain, while secretly hoping someone would notice and come rescue me from myself. I wanted God to see me—the only One I knew could make this all go away and wipe away my tears. But He never came. Or maybe He did and I was too deeply immersed in my struggles to notice Him standing next to me.

And I prayed.

I prayed for rescuing.

I prayed for clarity.

I prayed for guidance.

I prayed for the pain to go away.

I prayed for anything.

I prayed for something.

Nothing changed.

Things only continued to get worse.

So . . . I stopped praying.

I carried on with my life and turned my face away from the One who loves me most in this world. I blamed Him for my hurt. I blamed Him for my circumstances. I blamed Him for not being the One to come to me and for letting me walk away. All I could think about was how I act when someone I love gets upset with me. I don't let them walk away! Heck, I go out, buy them flowers, invite them to dinner, and make up. I make it right! Yet, here I was, walking along the road, alone, with nobody chasing after me.

For the first time in this fight, I was alone, and it was by choice. I was broken. I couldn't pray in church without having to persevere through an ocean of tears, so I stopped. I couldn't talk to my friends about His goodness without rolling my eyes, so I stopped. I couldn't speak to my father of confession without telling him how tired I was of seeking guidance, so I stopped.

Even though I was in the darkest of pits, fighting a losing battle with both my physical and mental health, my guilt worsened. I felt guilty for not having more control over my health and for allowing it to get that bad. But I also felt guilty that I was becoming a worse spouse and mother with each passing day. Things weren't improving, and I was sadly losing more of myself. I knew I had lost control, but the guilt held me back from admitting that to myself and my family.

So I continued to conceal the hurt for fear that they too would see how big a failure I was. The pain and anxiety had not only taken full control of my body; they were now very much in command of my mind. My heart was easily persuaded in the defeat of my body and mind and soon, the overwhelming sadness was all it could feel, to the point of pushing my loving God away. The guilt not only continued to encourage their reign, but the more control it allowed them, the more it grew. Any progress toward healing I made was quickly dampened by guilt's lies.

I started this chapter by telling you that we need to fill our lives with so much God that all our anxiety dissipates; yet, here I am telling you about how I did the exact opposite. I got to a point where I not only gave anxiety its own room, but I gave it everything—my entire house. I let it drive my one true Love out of my life, and I did nothing about it. Not only that, but I then got mad, expecting Him to come back and kick the anxiety out and make everything right again. I wanted Him to claim me again, even if it seemed against my will. I wanted Him to return, sweep me off my feet, and drive away my sadness. I expected something of His love that would essentially take away from its very essence: I wanted His love to remove my free will, the very thing He mercifully gave me from the start. He wanted me to want Him. He wanted me to return to Him willfully. He wanted me in my brokenness. But I told Him to leave—and then put the blame on Him.

This is what we do to God.

We get ourselves into the worst of messes and then make Him the reason for our downward slope. Yet He remains faithful. We kick Him out, asking Him to leave us alone, and then revel in disbelief that He actually left. Yet He waits only just down the road for us to call Him back. We shove Him into our box of desires, not giving Him free rein of our plans, and then blame Him when His entire ocean doesn't fit in the box with Him. Yet He remains merciful.

> "Through the Lord's mercies we are not consumed, because His compassions fail not. They are new every morning; great is Your faithfulness." ~ Lamentations 3:22–23

Even though I did this to Him, He was up to something. He was out crafting a plan to win my love back. God was out buying those flowers.

Don't get me wrong; none of this was under my control. But I continued to put the responsibility on God, and although I refused to get the help I needed initially, I still expected healing, and since that didn't come quickly, to me it meant that God wasn't coming. I couldn't feel Him tugging at my heart, thinking all I was getting from Him was radio silence.

The darkness really blinds us to the light. And although I blamed Him for my circumstances, deep in my heart, I knew I was the one who had to take the first steps out of my tomb. But I truly felt paralyzed by my hurt. Whatever progress I wished to make was further hindered by guilt.

Why does guilt have such a hold on us?

Every single female I've ever crossed paths with has expressed guilt for something completely out of her control. Even more confusing is that we multiply this guilt a millionfold once we become mothers. If we're a bit late for evening pickup or order takeout for dinner because didn't have time to cook, we beat ourselves up for months. And God forbid we want to take a moment for ourselves, to catch a breath from the uphill climb that is parenting!

I think we allow ourselves to feel guilty because our expectations for motherhood are skewed. When we are stuck on the idealistic and unattainable perfection discussed in the last chapter, of course we are going to feel guilty when we inevitably fall short of that standard. But we've established that our standard needs to be aligned with God's ultimate standard for our lives, and if He can use a donkey to deliver a message,[6] then He can surely use me to mother His children.

But that's the key: allowing Him to *use* me.

When I hand Him my life to do with as He wills, I am also handing Him my worries, fears, and failures to use for His bigger plan. And in doing that, the pressure is instantly lifted off my shoulders and into the hands of God. Suddenly, I realize that "by the grace of God I am what I am" (1 Corinthians 15:10) and that "[His] grace is sufficient for [me], for [His] strength is made perfect in weakness" (2 Corinthians 12:9).

Guilt will then subsequently fade away, no longer having the impact it once did on my life.

So, Mama, you're stuck in a spiral fueled by guilt, and I am right there with you, being sucked into its compelling vortex. But we need to hand our God that 'perfect' image of motherhood we have curated over the years and allow Him to use our shortcomings for His glory. In doing so, He rids us of the guilt that binds our limbs and covers our senses so that we can enjoy the beauty in this life He has given us.

Now look up!

Father,

You know the guilt that I harbor in my heart better than I do. But it continues to lead me down a relentless path, and it has become far too familiar. I am tired of fighting it for my happiness.

6. Read Numbers 22:22–28

Please hold my heart in Your hands and tend to it when it feels overwhelmed.

Allow the time spent in Your presence to be the healing I am so desperate for.

And cast out the guilt that continues to drive out Your peace.

Time to reflect . . .

1. List three things that you continually feel guilty for.

2. Now, write your strategies for combatting the guilt for each of the three things listed above.

3. Write a specific, short prayer that you can recite each time you feel guilt creeping up.

Is it me Lord?

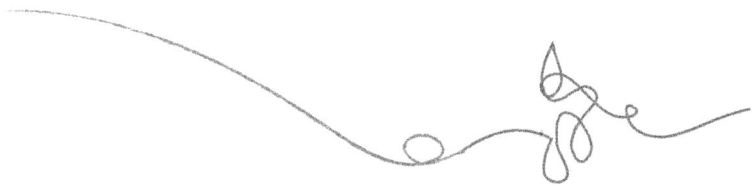

My story won't hit the box office if it were made into a film,
But it's a simple testimony on how God is faithful to those
who remain faithful to Him

– Patrick Baldwin

Chapter 3

Is It Me, Lord?

My story won't hit the box office if it were made into a film,

But it's a simple testimony on how God is faithful to those who remain faithful to Him.

—PATRICK BALDWIN

I wonder what motherhood was like for you;
you who brought the word 'mother' into existence

I wonder what your bad days looked like; you who always knew your worst day was yet to come

I wonder what you felt when He leapt inside you; you who carried the Creator of the World

I wonder what song your heart sang when He called you 'mom' for the first time; you who became mom to all humankind

I wonder how much pain you endured during labour; you who bore your Son's pain during His hour

I wonder if you didn't feel like enough for Him; you who

sustains everyone who searches for love

I wonder how much of our journeys we shared, even though you became a light to all who look to you at the end of yours

I wonder how much of my shortcomings, my failures, my insecurities you can relate to, even though you're a fortress of hope and a beacon of joy to all that come searching

I wonder if you look at me and think of how much more I can give, or you see how much of myself I've laid down

I wonder if you see the struggles, the tears, the cracks, and think that this is all part of it, or if there's something I'm missing

I wonder what it was like for you . . .

—Mirette Abraham, 2019

I wrote this while contemplating a beautiful little painting I purchased from Greece that depicts St. Mary, the mother of God, holding her hands out as Christ takes His first steps as a toddler. I was overcome with emotion as soon as it captured my attention in the store. I couldn't look away, and the image slowly went out of focus as my eyes welled up. My daughter was only twelve months old at that point and had just begun walking properly when we took her to Europe—the same age as My Lord in that image. I was at a point in my relationship with God where I was giving Him the silent treatment. I almost expected that by letting my hurt fester, He would sweep in overnight, realizing how much His silence had pained me, and He would make everything better again. I was at a point where I was well and truly walking the road alone (well, that's how I saw it anyway), but I couldn't help looking over my shoulder every so often to see if He was running toward me to claim me as His. I couldn't stand being spoken to about Him, and I couldn't swallow being given advice on how to 'get out' of my current situation. I wasn't in a 'situation,' but I felt as though I was in my new role as a mom in a strange new life without God. I couldn't see Him through all the pain that clouded my vision and mind.

There's a great line in a movie called *The Shack*—which follows a man on his journey of healing and rediscovering his faith after the death of his youngest daughter—when God answers the main character's question of "Where were You?" with, "Son, when all you see is your pain, you lose sight of Me."

Hearing His answer, I questioned, "Is that true, Lord? Were You actually there those nights where I was hunched over under the weight of my sadness, and all I could hear was the deafening noise of my own cries?"

As beautiful as that movie line is, it filled me with more questions than answers. Why wouldn't He just provide me with what I *needed* in that very moment, rather than just 'being there,' hoping I would turn to Him and ask for help? Why wouldn't He calm the storm raging inside me for so long, tearing through everything I built for myself, rather than wait for me to wake Him up amidst it? Why couldn't He just spare me all this hurt and fix it already? What was He waiting for? How much worse could it get before He decided I had suffered enough?

> "Many are the afflictions of the righteous, but the Lord delivers him out of them all." ~ Psalms 34:19

Maybe that was the problem.

Maybe I wasn't righteous.

Or maybe I wasn't holding up my end of the deal—appreciating that the Lord was doing what He had promised.

I can see this reflecting on it now, but hindsight is always 20/20. Back in the trenches, all I could see was my pain. I couldn't even make out the silhouette of the Lord eagerly awaiting my beckon. I couldn't see the countless bouquets He was leaving by my bedside, hopelessly expecting my thank-you note. My self-absorption blinded me so that I couldn't see I was the one digging myself further into my pit. My cries were so deafening that I wasn't able to hear all the voices of rescuers trying to pull me out. I couldn't see anything but myself.

On one of my shifts during this time, I walked into the ward, avoiding eye contact with any staff member who would recognize me so I could finish my round as quickly as possible. The weekend rounds were like the most intense game of Russian Roulette; you hope to God with every fiber of your being that you don't get shot with an unwell patient, because even one meant death to your entire weekend. While that was my attitude before heading out to work that morning, God made sure I didn't have that same outlook by the end of the shift. At the end of the corridor, I saw a man in a long, black robe. I would recognize that black robe and attire anywhere; it was one of our Coptic Orthodox priests! I felt such happiness seeing him at work. Even though I didn't know him, it was such a familiar comfort. Having him at my workplace automatically blessed my day. I bounced up to greet him—no longer taking notice of how many people in the ward spotted me—and asked for his prayers as I completed my round. "Ah, how fortunate," I thought to myself as I continued my work, "nothing can bring me down now!" I carried on, no longer so obsessed with finishing in a timely manner, rather just trying to be as thorough as possible so that all the patients got the care they deserve. I felt as though I were being looked after and giving my patients anything less than that same feeling would deny them their basic right as my patient.

I returned to the ward (I still can't remember why, as I'm pretty sure I had finished my work prior to returning) and ran into an older gentleman in the corridor. I didn't know him, but he seemed so pleased to see me that he couldn't help but offer me the most beaming and enthusiastic smile I had seen that day, almost as if I had the answers he was looking for.

"My daughter needs you," he managed. English was not his native tongue, so he struggled through the conversation. "Please talk to her."

"Of course, anything!" I replied, not knowing what I'd find behind the curtain.

She was broken—young, about my age, recently separated from her husband, caring for two young children on her own, and plagued with an illness that claimed her entire body. No medications were helping, and she was falling so deep into her own sadness that she tried to take matters into her own hands. She overdosed. She just wanted the pain to go away. But it didn't work. So, she did it again and again, each time landing in hospital for monitoring, rehydration, and counseling, only to find herself back again a few weeks later.

"What is it you want?" I asked, afraid of the answer.

"I don't want the pain." I wondered whether she only meant the physical ailment she was experiencing, or if she wanted to escape the unseen torment of her thoughts and hurt by ending her life. She continued before I could think of a delicate way to ask, "I never wanted to die, I just wanted something to get rid of this pain." The doctor in me didn't believe her—I had heard this multiple times from patients just trying to leave the hospital; once they deny those thoughts, it is quite hard to hold them against their will, even when you suspect the worst—but the struggling mom in me did.

I believed she wanted to be better for her children and that she was already hurting from thoughts of inadequacy and self-doubt, that the pain she was in only exaggerated this further. I believed she didn't want to end her life but that she wanted to amputate all the negative roots that were grounding her in a place of sheer agony. She wanted to run away with everything that she had.

But she couldn't. She didn't know how.

I knew this feeling all too well.

"I hear you," I said through tears. "I know you. And I am you! We can help each other. Let's talk."

At the wedding of Cana, our Lord asked the servants to partake in the miracle He was about to perform.

> "Jesus said to them, 'Fill the water pots with water.' And they filled them up to the brim. And He said to them 'Draw some out now, and take it to the master of the feast.' And they took it." ~ John 2:7–8

In honesty, I never noticed the servants' part until I read this chapter with a devotional. There were six of those pots to fill—large, heavy, stone pots. Imagine being asked to fill some large pots with water when the problem at hand was not a lack of water but a lack of wine. Imagine then, after filling these pots with water, being asked to give said water to the master of the feast! You know what you've poured into these pots. You know that what will come out is tasteless, normal water. You know that giving it to the master is a big deal, and you are likely to be thrown out of the wedding if what you deliver is not the wine he requested. But you do it anyway—without question, complaint, or amendments.

How often do we give God 'suggestions' about how He should do things in our lives? We approach God in prayer as though He is a genie, trapped in our little flask, providing us with exactly what we want at exactly the time we want it. We are telling God that we know better, that we can do better. We squeeze Him for a couple of sparkles when all He wants to do is give us the entire box of glitter. We stand before Him and adorn Him with our words, but we never surrender our hearts.

These servants didn't do that. They gave Him everything. They obeyed to the point of their expected shame and public humiliation. Even more beautiful, they filled the pots to "the brim," so that their love for the Lord not only filled their own emptiness but overflowed onto all who would witness this miracle and read about it for centuries to come. Their obedience and faith in the Lord rather than the outcome became a lighthouse to people searching for generations to come. Their example became the standard by which we should now hold ourselves to.

How much have I been filling my pot? I know it hasn't been to the brim, but does it even come close? What would filling it to the brim even look like for me?

Christ wanted those servants to not only watch the miracle but be a part of the miracle. That's what God wants for us. He can easily do what needs to be done without even acknowledging our existence in the matter. But He doesn't. He involves us, and in doing so, He transforms us too. We need to go through the motions, climb the hills, manage through the rain, persevere through the storm, pick ourselves up after we fall, and push through the pain to see the miracles unravel throughout the journey, bringing us closer to our destination: perfection. There, He will wait for us, excited to show us who we have become through it all, how by allowing us to partake in His work, we are transformed and renewed.

> "Therefore, if anyone is in Christ, he is a new creation; old things have passed away; behold, all things have become new." ~ 2 Corinthians 5:17

So maybe this was the missing part of my equation, the reason I couldn't solve the problem—me. I needed to be involved, to be part of the ultimate transformation.

I started "praying" again, or for lack of a better description, reading from my prayer book. I prayed when I least wanted to. I prayed when I couldn't keep my eyes open. I prayed every night. I didn't start with much, just two psalms and the "Our Father." I was in no place mentally to pour out my heart to God again. I was still hurting, and every time I tried to tell Him what I was feeling, I cried and shut myself off again. I would end my prayers with, "You know what I want" and walk away.

During this long and arduous uphill climb, God kept sending me gentle reminders He was busy working a greater thing within me. He sent me patients wanting to be served as little love notes. He sent me patients wanting to be tended to in death as flowers. He sent me constant reminders that I am His and I am here for a reason. And ultimately, He shook me out of my sadness and awakened me with the need for love—they all needed love, and I had to muster the courage to give it. I needed Him, Love Himself, to fill me before I tried to give from my negative supply. So, I prayed more fervently, praying for them to find hope in Him. I prayed for Him to use me as a vessel, to transport all this love and help them fill their own jars as well.

I know I didn't help that patient who overdosed, but she does not know how much she helped me. She made me realize I wasn't alone. There is so much beauty in the way God uses women to strengthen one another through His divine love, hope for a better tomorrow, and the promise of a healed yesterday.

To the mom reading this, or for those who resonate with the words on these pages amidst a state of chaos, know that you are being heard, and you are loved beyond comprehension.

God doesn't want to just wipe away your tears; He is collecting every one of them to water the life-nourishing soul He planted in you at the beginning.

God isn't waiting around the corner for you to stumble upon Him on your tumultuous journey; He has been right beside you, picking up the pieces of you that keep falling and building a mighty warrior out of them to protect His children everywhere.

God isn't speaking to you right now not because He isn't there but because He is listening attentively to your pain. When you stop and close your eyes, you will hear Him speak His love to you ever so gently.

God seems so distant right now not because space separates the two of you but because hurt does, and He is slowly turning that same hurt into your biggest strength.

God is creating for Himself a glorious and marvelous being in you. All you have to do is pour yourself out before Him so He can fill you with His might.

But you must actively pour.

You need to become an active part of healing.

God wants you. As you are.

And whether or not you believe it, you are His one and only.

You were deliberately created with specific intent for a particular purpose. And you are the only one of you!

You are worthy of love because Love created you.

Now, what is it He is asking of you this minute?

How can you take part in this miracle of rediscovery?

The answer to those questions will come when you stand before God and ask Him. Then, "whatever He says to you, do it" (John 2:5). That is simply my end of the deal. In rediscovering who I am and why I'm here, I need to ask God what He needs me to do—and then actually do it. He might ask something seemingly simple at the start, like just making the time to come into His presence daily and soak in His love. But that task might become more difficult as the refining progress—"He sit[s] as a refiner and purifier of silver" (Malachi 3:3)—so we need to be prepared for the fire. Or, like me, you might be in the midst of your fire right now and the hard task you're being asked to do is actually to just show up. But you and I both know that showing up can seem near impossible and trying to find the strength to lift yourself out of the darkness can be unimaginable.

So, Mama, we need to pray for clarity. And once we discover what it is the Lord wants from us, we need to pray for the strength to carry through with it.

Now look up!

Father,

Today, I commit to coming into Your presence daily.

Allow the time I spend with You to provide the clarity I need on this journey and tell me what it is You want from me.

Show me how and where You need me.

I know it'll be difficult and sometimes agonizing but give me the strength I need to fill those heavy, back-breaking pots.

I want to do my part, and I know now that I need to rediscover who I was created to be and what it is You require me to do in this life.

Time to reflect . . .

1. What is it you think the Lord is asking of you today?

2. As difficult as it seems, how will you practically take the steps to do it?

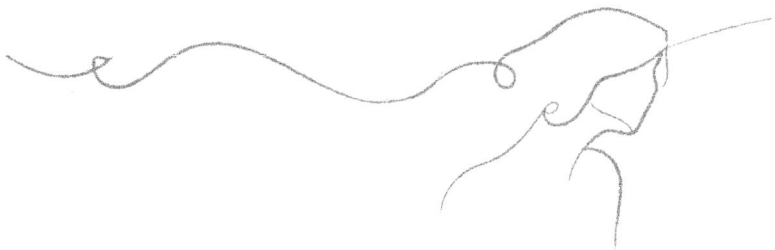

"God sees you not only as a mortal being on a small planet who lives for a brief season – He sees you as His child. He sees you as the being you are capable and designed to become. He wants you to know that you matter to Him."

— Dieter F. Uchtdorf

Chapter 4

Unseen

God sees you not only as a mortal being on a small planet who lives for
a brief season—He sees you as His child. He sees you as the being you
are capable and designed to become. He wants you to know that you
matter to Him.

—DIETER F. UCHTDORF

HAVE YOU EVER WONDERED if God really sees us? Like really sees
us—in all of our filth and with all of our baggage? Does He see
but then turn away, almost in shame, as though this is not how it's
supposed to look? Do you think He sees but then stands looking
pitifully at His creation, as though our lives are not meant to be a
melody of melancholy but full of love and joy? Or does He see and
just do nothing about it?

I ride this thought train far too often. I can't help but think
that He doesn't see me with all my questions and hurt. And sometimes I catch myself thinking how He most definitely sees but
likely doesn't care. I wave those thoughts away, though, because
that's not my God.

My God sees.

My God cares.

Growing up, I was always closer to my dad. I was, and still am, the epitomized stereotype of a "Daddy's Girl." He always knew exactly what was wrong when I would leave the room with a frown, and he knew exactly what to say when I was hurting and didn't want to talk about my feelings. He also never knew how to say "no" to me and struggled not to give me whatever ridiculous thing I asked of him. My mom was different. I felt like I could never make her happy, almost as if she constantly expected more of me even when I gave my absolute all. To me, we were dichotomous personalities. She didn't know me, and I couldn't read her. The worst part about our relationship was that neither of us was good at apologizing (until recently, I struggled to say "sorry" when I meant it but had no problem apologizing to a wall if I walked into it by accident).

I remember a particular incident when she made fun of how messy I was in front of my uncle. I don't remember the exact event, but I distinctly remember feeling betrayed by my mother. How could she reveal something so private (apparently that was my most shameful secret at the time, although everyone else knew full well how messy I was)? How could she laugh at me and make fun of me like that?

I was a young teenager and, like any young female "adult," I had trouble loving my mother and seeing her in the light of all the sacrifices she made for us each day and just how much of herself she poured out for us to feel filled. I almost looked for reasons to blame her for the way I was (or wasn't) handling all the changes occurring in my own life. I wanted to find any excuse to keep pushing her further away, afraid that the closer she got, the better she would be at fixing all my problems, just as she had continually solved everything for everyone. This was my time to figure things out, and I didn't want her and all her wisdom getting involved.

The thing that upset me so much that day was that she never apologized to me. It was my dad who came into my room and made things right when he had nothing to do with it! He just hated conflict and needed to make sure everyone was happy at all times. That day drove an even larger wedge between my mother and me.

I never spoke to her about my struggles with friends.

I never spoke to her about boys.

I never spoke to her about my true aspirations.

I never spoke to her about my mistakes—or how to fix them.

We just never really spoke. And that wasn't her fault; that was mine. Maybe I was afraid of judgement. I'll never be sure, but I always attributed our not speaking to her lack of interest in my life—her lack of interest in me.

My perspective changed once I became a mother. The first and only person I shared my pains with and completely poured myself out to was my mom. We went furniture shopping one Saturday, just the two of us. On the way back, while I was driving, she turned to me and asked, "Are you okay?"

I don't know why that was a trigger for me, or why I cried the way I did. Maybe it was because nobody, not a single person, had asked me that question in the year prior. Nobody had even noticed how much I was hurting and, worse, how much I had changed from the person I once was. I had worked so hard to conceal my pain, to keep people in the dark for as long as I could to figure all this out and get over this thing that had claimed my personality.

I cried and cried. For what felt like a lifetime. Once I started, the floodgates just shattered open and let out the entire bank of tears I had invested over the past year. I finally managed, "No, but I don't know why." We spoke the entire way back, and she told me so many stories about her own upbringing and struggles, constantly bringing up Christ's love for me and how He only longs for my joy to be found in Him. If I had to pinpoint the moment that I started my crawl back to God, I would have to say it was that day. Sitting in that car with my mom, I felt her remove the weight that had set up camp on my shoulders. Piece by piece, the blocks came off and then vanished, as though she was taking them from me and handing them back to God to deal with. She was merely the bridge between me and my Lord, but without her, I could never have crossed over to meet Him.

There's a process in my work with patients called 'handover,' which takes place at the start of each shift—day, evening, and night. Its name basically summarizes its nature: both teams get together to hand over anything important from the previous shift along with any further tasks left to finish during the following shift. In this meeting, each doctor passes the baton to the next doctor covering their wards and patients, allowing them to go home without worrying about anything from their day. The task is someone else's problem to worry about and complete. Once you leave the handover, you no longer carry the burden of the outstanding tasks from your shift; you feel lighter knowing that someone else is now carrying that burden for you and will tackle it in a way they feel is right.

That's how I felt after my car ride with my mom; she had passed my burden on to God, and He will now deal with all of it in a way He feels is right for me. I was in safe hands. My mother truly saw me that day, even though I spent my entire childhood sure that she knew nothing about the daughter she had brought into this world. That day, she saw me in all of my hurt, and she knew me in all of my pain. The woman who once fought off the bullies at school, teaching them one heck of a lesson about who not to mess with, was now defending me in the face of all my adversaries. Not only that but she was sending them back to the One who can fix anything and, in doing so, began the tremendous task of my restoration.

She unraveled my load, so I didn't have to try to alone. She began lifting the things that had settled right at the top, pressing down on their counterparts below. She removed them from my shoulders and gave them to God, handing Him everything I was holding on to. And for the first time, I felt as though everything was going to be okay. For so long I had held on to everything out of fear that not doing so made me less of the mother He had intended when He made me. The more she removed, the more I realized I didn't know my Maker. I had carved an image of Him in my mind that did not fit His pure love. I had made Him into something He most definitely was not. His intention was never for me to be bogged down and burdened by the things that should bring me joy. His intention was for us to meet on this journey, but my focus had turned to my inabilities when my only focus should have been His extraordinary abilities. The more my mom lifted off, the clearer my mind and heart became. I could see myself again. I could see Him again. All because she took the time to help me with my load. All because she knew how to navigate her own experience through motherhood by directing everything she held dear to the One who loves her the most. She learned that He fixes and mends our wounds, but we need to let Him. She was showing me what I needed to do with my load that day, as well as all the burdens I continued to claim as my own.

Motherhood is a thankless job.

You're not just carrying your own load; you pick up the bits falling off everyone else's shoulders. You struggle under the weight of the baggage everyone feels they can unload on you, because in doing so, their pain eases and their load lightens. They're completely unaware of how little of your own load you will give to someone else, in fear that you will no longer be everyone's resting place. You hold on to it all, secretly praying for it to one day lighten on its own.

But it doesn't, and it won't—as long as you don't let go.

Instead, the load becomes a source of fear, of anger, and sometimes, of resentment.

You fear the person you are becoming with each passing day, letting go of the things you love, the things you find solace in, and the person you once were to make room for the ever-growing load above and within you.

You feel anger toward your inability to deal with everything rationally and unemotionally, thinking that once you became a mom you were supposed to have answers to everything for everyone, and being anything less than this fictional being, you are not enough.

You resent the lack of support offered to you, even though you make your battles as private as possible, unimpressed that nobody has read your mind and broken down the walls that harbor your mind and soul, holding you captive with your malignant load.

For the first time on my chaotic adventure, I felt seen. My mother saw beyond the facade, right through to the pain and the hurt. She saw my heart trying to explode out of the shell of expectations that had encased it for so long and my soul being crushed under a gigantic pile of emotionally triggering thoughts and worries. She saw me trying so hard to be someone I thought I needed to be—and trying even harder to hide how much it was killing me. She saw me and, in doing so, reminded me that God always sees me.

Mama, you are magnificent in any form that you are or become. The person you were is still the person you are, but you are stronger, wiser, and more fiercely loved than ever before! One day, the you who you knew before will make herself known again, but the mark you are leaving on this earth is unapologetically and inconceivably breathtaking.

Mama, you can do anything and everything, but becoming a fictional character curated from other people's expectations and judgment isn't the thing you should focus on. No matter how much you give to this image, it will continue to take from you; no matter how big your sacrifices, it will continue to expect more from you. This fictional being does not exist, and there isn't a single, uniform mold that could encapsulate every heroine of motherhood out there! We're all different and amazing in our own rights. And if you need confirmation of this, just focus on the starry-eyed gazes that follow you around your own living room.

Finally, Mama, you are feeling unsupported because your load is too heavy. You are a master at hiding your true role and worth. You are trying so hard to be the ultimate heroine, the one who saves everyone in the story, while concealing how much your own battle of finding self-worth continues to suffocate you. You run away from how little you think of yourself by completely immersing yourself in your family and your home. But what if you saw yourself the way God sees you? What would you see if you spent the day walking in your daughter's shoes looking up at yourself? What would you feel if you held your own hand and heart the way your husband does?

You don't know your worth because you refuse to see it under all the baggage you insist on carrying alone. But know that the way you see yourself is tainted by what the world expects of you.

You are enough in your sense of inadequacy. Because what you deem insufficient is actually an abundance of a love that has no bounds.

You are not alone in your thoughts of loneliness. We are all right there with you, sitting in the same crowded room, thinking we are walking this path on our own.

You are perfect in your imperfection. We crafted our ideas of perfection from the thoughts and ideas of people just like you and me, creating an unachievable and unrealistic standard. Know that the ultimate Absolute and the perfect God created you with His standard of perfection in mind, and He is quite pleased with His masterpiece—you.

> "Then God saw everything that He had made, and indeed it was very good." ~ Genesis 1:31

So, Mama, know that God sees you.

He sees those fears and doubts, and He wishes to relieve you of their burden, because He cares.

And He cares because He loves you.

Now look up!

Father,

Help me come to appreciate that You are on this path right beside me.

You see my struggles, my fears, my doubts, and my pain. And You care enough to carry me through them with Your peace.

Open my eyes so that I can see You and feel Your love while I continue to walk this road toward rediscovery and healing.

Time to reflect . . .

1. Do you occasionally feel invisible to your family and friends?

2. If your answer is "yes," when are you more likely to feel this way and what emotions or experiences does it stir up in you?

3. Think of a scriptural example where Christ proved His care. Write out how that encounter made you feel or what it made you believe of His character. Keep this handy, as it will remind you of who He is when you are feeling unseen.

You don't get
Lost in the Crowd

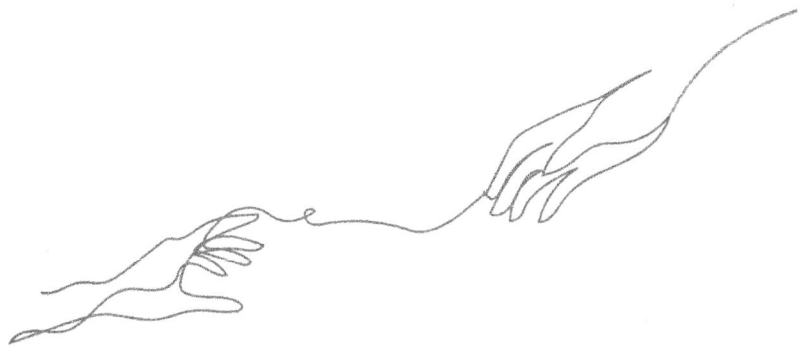

"*I* want you to live in confidence that when God looks at you, He sees beauty. He sees value. He sees hope. And that even when you're hiding, or when you're so beaten down you can't see anything clearly, He's still hard at work, crafting a beautiful future of relationship with Him and with others."

Tammy Maltby, The God Who Sees You: Look to Him When You Feel Discouraged, Forgotten, or Invisible

Chapter 5

You Don't Get Lost in the Crowd

I want you to live in confidence that when God looks at you, He sees beauty. He sees value. He sees hope. And that even when you're hiding, or when you're so beaten down you can't see anything clearly, He's still hard at work, crafting a beautiful future of relationship with Him and with others.

—TAMMY MALTBY, *THE GOD WHO SEES YOU*

WE DON'T GET LOST in the crowd. God sees us, and He wants to give us His whole heart, but we need to pursue Him. We need to get past everything that is trying to push us farther away from Him.

We need to block out the voice of self-doubt.

We need to silence the fear of not being seen.

We need to use our small, seemingly insignificant faith as the sole driving force to fuel our pursuit of restoration and desire for our Lord.

We need to hold fast to the truth of our Lord's unending love for us. A love that is pure and unconditional, knowing no bounds. Love that stretched His arms on a cross and laid down His life for us. Love that wants us as we are. He desires nothing in return but our own love and patiently waits for us to love Him back.

"Now a certain woman had a flow of blood for twelve years, and had suffered many things from many physicians. She had spent all that she had and was no better, but rather grew worse. When she heard about Jesus, she came behind Him in the crowd and touched His garment. For she said, 'If only I may touch His clothes, I shall be made well.' Immediately the fountain of her blood was dried up, and she felt in her body that she was healed of the affliction. And Jesus, immediately knowing in Himself that power had gone out of Him, turned around in the crowd and said, 'Who touched My clothes?' But His disciples said to Him, 'You see the multitude thronging You, and You say, "Who touched Me?"' And He looked around to see her who had done this thing. But the woman, fearing and trembling, knowing what had happened to her, came and fell down before Him and told Him the whole truth. And He said to her, 'Daughter, your faith has made you well. Go in peace, and be healed of your affliction.'" ~ Mark 5:25–34

Imagine the setting and envision her determination to be near Him.

It's crowded. No room to move past even the person closest to her.

She sees Him from afar, but the crowd continues to push her farther away.

He continues to move through the crowd, healing and blessing everyone in His path. But not her. She's too far away, losing hope of restoration with each passing minute. Soon enough, He'll be gone, taking her faith with Him.

This is it. This is the time for action.

She can't catch His gaze. She waves and yells hysterically, but He can't hear her.

"I must touch Him!" she thinks.

She crawls on the ground, hoping that she can evade the masses of people that way and avoid being pushed away from her Lord.

She sees His feet! She's finally going to reach Him!

"I just need the hem . . . that'll heal me."

Sweat dripping into her eyes, making her vision blur.

Her heart now beating a soft tune in her ears, making it impossible to hear anything above it.

But it doesn't matter. Because she's made it. She touches the hem of His garment and immediately she is restored. Her bleeding ceases, and her faith blooms new leaves.

"Who touched Me?" He asks aloud, bringing to her throat a lump of fear so large she can't speak.

He felt her. He mended her. She didn't get lost in the crowd. Instead, because of her perseverance in seeking Him and fighting for her healing, she was seen by Him.

His gaze of love falls upon her, and in an instant, He changes her forever.

God is something and someone specific to every character in the Bible. He also claims a very specific role in my own life, but I'm still figuring out exactly what that is.

Hagar was a young Egyptian maidservant for one of the most renowned female figures in the Old Testament: Sarah, Abraham's wife. Hagar doesn't occupy very much of the story in Genesis, but the pages that do mention her are not ones to be missed. Most people just know Hagar as Abraham's mistress or Ishmael's mother, but God saw her as so much more. If you're unfamiliar with the story, Sarah was barren and told Abraham to conceive a child through her maidservant, Hagar. Once Hagar found out she was pregnant, it seems she thought poorly of Sarah, so Sarah treated her harshly, driving Hagar to flee from her presence. While Hagar sat in the wilderness alone, an Angel of the Lord appeared and comforted her. Hagar then beautifully acknowledges her God as "the God who sees."

And cue one of my favorite verses in the Bible.

> "Then she called the name of the Lord who spoke to her,
> You-Are-the-God-Who-Sees; for she said, 'Have I also
> here seen Him who sees me?'" ~ Genesis 16:13

Jeremiah, too, while disputing with God about why the wicked prosper and anguishing in pain, proclaims that God sees him.

"But You, O Lord, know me; You have seen me."
~ Jeremiah 12:13

When we feel as though nobody sees us, we turn to something or someone who does—something we feel is going to hold us in higher regard than what we perceive we are missing from our relationship with others, and sadly, with God. We feel as though we are the lost sheep, but in our case, God isn't leaving the ninety-nine behind to come find us. We feel as though all we have to give is the two mites, but in our case, God expects more. We almost feel ignored and left to our own vices, so we search for something that will make us feel significant. But we aren't ever alone in this struggle, and we're definitely not the first to feel this way. Do you remember the account in Genesis of the Tower of Babel? The people wanted to build a tower that reached into the heavens, specifically to "make a name for [themselves]" (Genesis 11:4).

We search for something so that we can make a name for ourselves—how could anyone be invisible if the tower they build on earth reaches the heavens? We want people to notice us, see us, like us. We search for people's adoration wherever we turn because we feel invisible.

But God sees us. Whether or not we like it or believe it, He sees us.

He sees our fear; He sees our strength.

He sees our pain; He sees our joy.

He sees our anxiety; He sees our hope.

He sees our shortcomings; He sees our talents.

He sees us—every bit of us.

I need to look toward Him at all times, so the low points are not so devastating and so when I feel invisible, I remember all the times He showed Himself to be a force of love in my life.

There was one workout when I felt as though I had been running for ages! I could feel the floor beneath me sending pulses of fatigue up my legs, almost synchronized with the beating of my heart. The pounding in my chest was desperately trying to silence the beating my mind was getting. I tried to drown out the noise further by increasing the volume on my music, but the words only served as a reminder of my hurt. Throughout my journey thus far, I had never truly been alone with my thoughts. I kept tucking them further away, relentlessly trying to numb the pain rather than face it. I hid behind a fake smile, trying to convince not only others but myself that I was okay. I ran to my mom duties, thinking that the more preoccupied I became with my daughter and her needs, the less of my reality I had to face. And I buried my mind in work I didn't need to do, taking on additional services and projects in hopes of busying myself to the point of absolute mental fatigue, when my faculties could no longer take on the burden of paying attention to my problems—or so I thought.

I also thought physically running would solve the problem. But on that running track, where I was physically doing exactly what my mind and heart were trying to do for so long, I finally came face-to-face with the very fears that had landed me there.

I started running during the coronavirus pandemic in 2020. If you're reading this a few years down the line, when this period is a distant memory or you were too young to remember the year the entire world stood still, let me refresh your memory. Simply put, one guy ate a bat, which was infected with a virus. He then got very ill and infected everyone he encountered. Being such early days (and nobody predicting a pandemic), everyone went on about their days and lives as normal—in doing so, they too infected everyone they encountered. Fast-forward to 2020, and the entire world is on lockdown. You're only allowed to leave the house for work (if you can't work from home), to get groceries for your family, to exercise outdoors and alone, or to seek medical attention. The beautiful thing about that year is that we were all forced to strip away everything keeping us from a relationship with God, and it left us in our homes finally alone with our Father. The sad thing, though, is that this alone time for some was spent in fear, not knowing when their next paycheck would come or how they would put food on the table for their children that day. The stillness stirred up anxiety, and the quiet stripped away many of the things we need for survival. I wish I could tell you a pleasant story about a family who saw miracle after miracle because of their reliance on God rather than their jobs.

But I can't.

People became so anxious they turned away from God and contemplated throwing in the towel on life altogether.

As much as people like to see this period as everyone being in the same boat and learning to survive by getting together and coming up with new and creative ways to pass the time, this wasn't the case.

We were all affected by the same struggle, but we did not struggle the same.

The quiet for some was a time to reconnect with family and rediscover hobbies they swept under the rug. But for most, this was a time to survive with minimal resources. Single parents lost their jobs. Abusive partners were constantly home and bored. Depressed teenagers were taken away from the friends and sports that once gave them purpose.

The flood waters were quickly eliminating those who couldn't stay afloat with the things they had, or who couldn't swim because they never learned.

But somehow, God continued to use this period for good. I have no doubt that I will hear more about those who thought they had drowned, only to be pulled up at the last minute, gasping for air and giving thanks. More and more people are finally hearing God's voice in the silence. We have silenced the busyness of the morning work rush. We have silenced the noise surrounding bedtime. We have stopped fretting about the outfits we need to buy for the many events coming up. We have spent so much time at home that our dishes have piled up, but the laundry has decreased. We haven't thought about our weight, our image, or the way people perceive us because we have stopped objectifying ourselves through their eyes. We have spent our mornings in prayer, our afternoons in contemplation, and our evenings being still in His presence. It forced us to rely on the Giver of gifts, rather than the gifts themselves. We have read about Him again and have been getting to know our Bridegroom, and we are finally preparing for our union with Him.

Personally, the pandemic forced me to sit still and stripped away everything I was using to escape from myself. Service has ceased, mindless coffee chats have ended, and all the busyness that filled each day has turned to silence. I had nothing left to help me hide from my truth, and I finally found myself in a room, alone with my thoughts. I picked up running as a last resort to escape that void; I had become accustomed to running away. I thought maybe if I was physically running, I could keep up with the fake persona I had created.

But running did the opposite.

The pulses that traveled up my body with each long stride awakened my heart, and soon enough, its palpable hurt was impossible to ignore. The more fatigued my legs became, the more my heart finally surrendered. So, I continued to run, and as I ran, I became more attentive to the cries it was forcing out. I heard my heart for the first time in years. I listened to everything it had harbored for so long and finally gave it the space it deserved. With every run I went on, more tears flowed.

I cried not only over how much I was hurting, but over how I let it get to this point. I denied for so long while God continued to tug at my heart. Even in the middle of a pandemic, when the entire world was thrown into confusion and disarray, my Lord didn't forget me. Much like the woman who was healed of her many years of bleeding, I didn't get lost in the crowd.

No matter how deep I was in the sea of despair of people around me, God still saw me. He sent His love surging through my body to pierce my heart so that I had no choice but to recognize Him standing there, begging me to take His hand.

I am finding Him again. I spent so long running away from Him and wondering why He wasn't running after me. I've finally returned to the road home, and I can see Him making His way hastily toward me; I can feel His excitement in every step I continue to take in His direction. And with each of my small, hesitant steps,

He continues to run with love and purpose, making the distance I have to walk shorter with each leap. But I keep stopping in hesitation, running over bumps filled with questions about those around me not having this experience. Does God see all the bruises from the beatings and blows that keep striking them down? Is God doing anything to make navigating through this new and unfamiliar terrain any easier? Does God even see their struggles? How can we all acknowledge Him with Hagar as "the God who sees"? I look around to see who else has been in the crowd, searching for someone to notice, but I struggle.

I don't have the answers to those questions, but I do have the solution for our peace. In every scenario, it is Christ. David says in his psalms, "those who trust the Lord are like mount Zion, which cannot be moved, but abides forever" (Psalms 125:1). Mount Zion never changes, regardless of the climate. But my faith is more comparable to a leaf, blowing so swiftly with any direction the wind takes it. I need to make my faith be the overcomer of each of my fears. I want this period in our lives to be a memory of a time when our faith was as unshakable as Mount Zion—so that we can come out of the fire with the three young youths unscathed, so that we can come out of the den with Daniel unharmed, so that we can emerge on the other side victorious, knowing that our God is the same God who delivered Job, Joseph, Moses, and all the greats. I wish we could see that He is walking this journey with us, holding us close, and all He asks in return is for us to trust in His glory and grace and know that nothing is out of His control!

How can I be afraid of anything when I have that same God as my own Father?

So, Mama, if you feel as though you are in the sea of people struggling to catch a break, or if you feel your anxiety has kept you from making your way through the masses to our Savior, know that you have been found. You may not feel His power surge through you instantly, but keep looking up and continue focusing on Him. You will find each other. And no crowd, big or small, can stop that.

Now look up!

Father,

Help me use this hard time as a time to reconnect with You and rekindle the fire in our relationship.

Help me use this time to help my fellow brethren in their struggles and be that arm that helps You pull them out of the flood water.

Help me use this time to pray for those who cannot see You past their own hurt.

Help me use this time to reclaim my faith and use it as a beacon of hope for those who are struggling to find their way home.

Help us get through this together, and don't leave us to try to swim on our own.

Help us see You, as Hagar so eloquently described, as the God who sees us.

Lord, You see us and love us so clearly and so deeply. Now help us see You and love You the same.

Time to reflect . . .

1. If you were affected by the pandemic, what has that meant for you? List the positives (if any) and all the negatives of that period. Now, beside the positives, write a prayer of gratitude, and beside the negatives, write a prayer expressing how they are making you feel and what you are asking of our Lord to improve things for you.

2. How can we use isolation and silence to meet our Maker?

3. List a few practical things you can do each day to allow yourself the space and silence to hear our Lord.

A heart made
to love

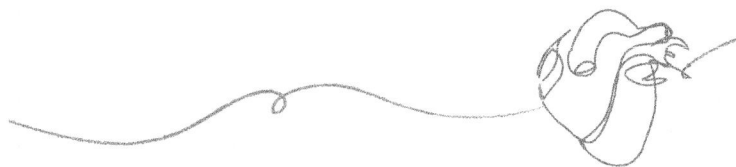

"*O*h Father, my Father... Father God."
Hesitantly, I spoke His name aloud.
I tried different ways of speaking to Him.
And then, as if something broke through for me
I found myself trusting that He was indeed hearing
me, just as my earthly father had always done.

"Father, O my Father God," I cried, with growing
confidence. My voice seemed unusually loud in the
large bedroom as I knelt on the rug beside my bed.
But suddenly that room wasn't empty anymore.
He was there! I could sense His Presence.
I could feel His hand laid gently on my head.
It was as if I could see His eyes, filled with love
and compassion. He was so close that I found
myself laying my head on His knees like a little girl
sitting at her father's feet.
For a long time I knelt there, sobbing quietly,
floating in His love.
I found myself talking with Him,
apologising for not having known Him before.
And again came His loving compassion,
like a warm blanket settling around me

I Dared to Call Him Father.
The miraculous Story of a Muslim
Woman's Encounter with God.

By Bilquis Sheikh with Richard H. Schneider.

Chapter 6

A Heart Made to Love

"Oh Father, my Father . . . Father God."

Hesitantly, I spoke His name aloud. I tried different ways of speaking to Him. And then, as if something broke through for me I found myself trusting that He was indeed hearing me, just as my earthly father had always done.

"Father, O my Father God," I cried, with growing confidence. My voice seemed unusually loud in the large bedroom as I knelt on the rug beside my bed. But suddenly that room wasn't empty anymore.

He was there!

I could sense His Presence. I could feel His hand laid gently on my head. It was as if I could see His eyes, filled with love and compassion. He was so close that I found myself laying my head on His knees like a little girl sitting at her father's feet. For a long time I knelt there, sobbing quietly, floating in His love. I found myself talking with Him, apologizing for not having known Him before. And again came His loving compassion, like a warm blanket settling around me.

—BILQUIS SHEIKH WITH RICHARD H. SCHNEIDER,
I DARED TO CALL HIM FATHER

LET'S, JUST FOR A MINUTE, look at the lady who anointed the feet of Jesus in the gospels.

"Then, six days before the Passover, Jesus came to Bethany, where Lazarus was who had been dead, whom He had raised from the dead. There they made Him a supper; and Martha served, but Lazarus was one of those who sat at the table with Him. Then Mary took a pound of very costly oil of spikenard, anointed the feet of Jesus, and wiped His feet with her hair. And the house was filled with the fragrance of the oil. But one of His disciples, Judas Iscariot, Simon's son, who would betray Him, said, 'Why was this fragrant oil not sold for three hundred denarii and given to the poor?' This he said, not that he cared for the poor, but because he was a thief, and had the money box; and he used to take what was put in it. But Jesus said, 'Let her alone; she has kept this for the day of My burial. For the poor you have with you always, but Me you do not have always.'" ~ John 12:1–8

I often wonder how she felt leading up to that moment.

She knew exactly what criticism awaited her behind those doors, yet her eyes focused on her one, true Love. Imagine the preparation that went into this beautiful encounter!

For months she would have had to put money aside to purchase the costly flask of fragrance and think of the perfect expression of her love for Him. Back in those days, everybody wore open sandals, and their feet inevitably were muddy by the end of the day after being exposed to the dirt floors and the elements. It is the custom of Jews to wash before meals, and Jesus had most likely washed His feet prior to sitting at that table. They would have been clean, but they probably still smelled of the day's work. She would have planned to wash that exact part of Him with her most prized possession to prove a single point: her love for her Savior stretched beyond her comfort and pride. She spilled her entire heart through that flask onto the least desirable part of His body and proceeded to wipe His feet with the very hairs on her head, setting aside her own pride and glory for the sake of love. She poured her whole heart on that floor before Him, without hesitation or fear of ridicule. And in return for her perfect love, our Lord raised her memory and legacy up the ranks, so that we are all now striving to emulate that same expression of love for our God.

But I constantly fall short of that perfect expression.

I remember a particular patient of mine who I cared for a short while back, his face etched into my memories forever. I hated him. I don't use that word often, but I couldn't stand going into his room, trying to care for him as best as I could, only to hear how I wasn't doing my job well and how his level of care was suboptimal. I guess he might have been right; maybe my frustrations were more apparent than I thought. But I hated being told to be better while I spent my days pouring out my entire soul and strength into my job. It struck a nerve hearing that I wasn't enough for him.

One day he seemed different.

Before I walked in that day, I heard him sobbing.

I saw the tears rolling down his cheeks and soaking through his bed sheets. He wasn't the same arrogant, selfish man I wanted to avoid before. He was broken, struggling to find his place in a world that would soon end for him. That day, he was a shell of the man I thought I knew. I had judged him based on what I deemed acceptable—what would cause me the least discomfort and add the least amount of work to my plate. I wanted him to be someone else, to make me more comfortable.

But Christ never did that.

He didn't turn away the tax collector because his profession was shameful; instead, He asked him to join Him on His journey and called him "friend."

He didn't turn away the woman at the well because culture dictated; instead, He restored her and used her to spread His good news.

He didn't turn away the adulteress when she courageously anointed Him, not knowing what fate awaited her; instead, He embraced her, ensured her name was written in history for all to see, and used her as an example of love for all to emulate.

In that moment, in my patient's vulnerability, I saw just how inattentive I had been to the crying of his heart.

He longed for companionship, and I had done my best to escape his bedside each morning.

He longed for someone to hear his fears, and I had done my best to shove my ideologies down his throat without taking the time to listen.

He longed for love, but I gave him none.

Seeing his sadness, I wept for my lack of love.

I walked into this profession vowing to show people Christ and bring them His love; yet, here I was doing the exact opposite of what He had sent me out to do.

I dragged my feet to my patient's bedside, half expecting to be criticized or asked to leave him alone. But I would not leave. I had to make up for lost time, and we had a lot of catching up to do.

He said nothing. I don't even think he noticed me coming in. He was so engulfed in his pain that it had wrapped itself around his senses, making him oblivious to anything else. Pain has a way of silencing everything else and centers itself in a way that allows everything to revolve around it, making you unable to focus your heart and mind on anything else in your life.

I knelt and held his hand; he needed to know I was finally there to listen to him and to show him the love I had selfishly withheld all this time. Soon enough, it all came pouring out—his fear of dying, his estranged children, his previous belief in God, and how he thought it was too late for him. His anxiety stirred up similar questions in me: Could this truly be how it all ended for him, without being surrounded by hope or love? Had God turned His back on him because he denied Him first?

Not my God.

My God anxiously waits for me at my favorite coffee shop every day, orders my regular, and sits there until the day draws to a close, hoping one of these days I'll show up to talk to Him.

My God had been excitedly expecting this very moment.

He was knocking furiously on the door of this man's heart, hoping the day would come when he would remember His love and mercy and ask Him to come back into his life.

No, it wasn't too late. It was perfectly timed so that not only his soul would find rest, but my soul would also learn how to love again and find restoration in that very moment.

I spent that afternoon making a few phone calls and getting a social worker involved—all the while praying that we could find his family. We found a few contact numbers and addresses, but nobody answered our calls. We both left voice messages asking them to come to the ward the next day to visit, explaining that this was his single wish. The hope that sparked within me had faded by the end of the day. I didn't know if he was going to get to see his family before he left this earth. But it comforted me to know that he had sought God again, and as hastily as He does, God came running to him that day, embraced him, and brought his soul back home.

To my surprise, upon my arrival the following morning, they were there—his two children and his wife—sitting by his side, laughing, and sharing memories.

The family he hadn't seen in over ten years was sitting beside him.

The family he criticized right out of his life was there.

Love was there.

God was there.

And I got to bear witness to it all. God allowed me to be part of this man's journey of repentance so that I too could remember what I was called to do on this road. I needed to remember who to love, and I needed to learn how to love.

A short while later, I was being criticized again. But that time, I didn't mind.

We spend our entire lives searching for something to fill the gaping holes in our hearts—holes caused by all the hurt, the pain, the people seeking to tear us down. But they remain holes because of us. We tend to the wounds with a lack of faith, hopelessness, despair, and reminders of all our other pains. We pour more fuel to keep the fire of restlessness alight. We know that running to our Maker will surely put it out, but it's almost like we enjoy wallowing in our hurts so that we don't lose the memories attached to them.

We don't want to replace our empty frame with new photos for fear that in doing so, we are also replacing the happiness that once occupied that same space. We hold on to our old and ragged possessions, hesitant to throw them out or give them to others for fear that in doing so, we are also throwing away the joy that came when we first got them. We store our deepest fears and most hurtful moments in a suitcase within our hearts and minds for fear that letting them go would mean losing a piece of ourselves. But life continues to throw punches. It continues to add more pain. And the more we hoard in our hearts, the more holes we allow it to create. Soon enough, the number of holes outnumber the intact spots. We allow the hoard to claim our hearts. We give it free rein of our most sacred place—the place that should belong to our God.

Some of these spaces represent who we once were.

Inevitably, our experiences, much like our trials, change us.

We change with each chapter we finish, and each chapter must end to make way for the next one. Yet, we fret turning the page for fear that in doing so, we let go of the person we were while reading that last paragraph. We get caught up in the emotional roller coaster and finally catch a breath only when we realize it led us to a state of pure joy. But we know that the next chapter, like the last one, starts quite rough.

It throws us curveballs while it twistingly leads us to our destination.

It causes fountains of tears that start with the anxious anticipation that rides on each page turn, finally ending in relief.

We know all too well how the story goes, but we can't know how it ends unless we immerse ourselves in its narrative.

But we hold on.

We struggle with the thought of letting go of our creativity to make way for organized chaos.

We can't fathom giving up our personal space to make way for nights and years of sharing pillows.

We lose sight of the bliss that awaits us because we can't picture anything more joyful than the moments passed.

God continues to tug at our comforts to help us make way for the new. He wants us to feel joy no matter what chapter we're on. The only thing He asks of us is to trust Him and let ourselves go.

But how God? This is who I am! This is who I know myself to be!

Have you ever been in the middle of one of the biggest storms of your life, constantly wondering how you'll ever get out the other side, and the next minute notice you're suddenly standing on war-torn fields, trying to rebuild a life from the embers that remain? When tirelessly rebuilding, usually our only thought is how exhausted we are, how there's no way we can keep going—we have nothing left of ourselves to give. But just as we are about to give up, we stand up and notice we haven't just rebuilt the house we will live in; we've built an entire neighborhood filled with all the virtues that'll fuel our unpredictable road ahead. We are filled with joy and a sense of accomplishment and pride that could only have come through our perseverance and reliance on Him who can do everything!

Now forget that impossible feat you thought you would never overcome. Just think about the book in your hands that you need to keep reading—but you're stuck on that last chapter, hesitant to flip the page.

Now take a deep breath and turn that page.

That's all He asks of us.

He wants us to keep reading—to keep riding the waves of uncertainty, fear, and darkness so that we can make it to the garden of His joy.

Along the way, we will want to stop. I've stopped. But in that stillness and quiet is not the peace we were hoping to get. Instead, that stillness, that pause, gives that anxiety further room to fester, without the distraction of the adventure that awaits.

So, don't stop.

That patient of mine had every reason to stop. He had every excuse to close that book right there and then and wait for death while giving his heart over to his sorrow.

But God didn't let him.

God kept tugging at his soul to reopen that book and continue searching for the hope he thought he had lost. He kept poking at him with His love, reminding him that even though he turned his back on Him, He was still walking right beside him, badgering him to trust just one last time.

So, he took a breath and reopened the book. And in doing so, his heart, once filled with gaping holes too large for repair, became a vessel of love and hope.

Mama, we may not like that the holes have occupied major real estate in our hearts and minds. But what we cannot see is the amount of light that can now easily penetrate those gaps.

By letting more of ourselves go, we give God more room to show.

Now look up!

Father,

I get stuck on the holes in my heart from all the hurt I have experienced, seeing them as flaws and nothing more. I see them as the reason I feel unworthy, imperfect, and unloved.

But Lord, I cannot see the light trying to shine through them, because I continually try to conceal them from the world.

You see them as a way of reflecting Your light onto everyone I cross paths with.

People see my holes, but instead of seeing flaws, they are filled with hope, knowing they are seen and loved by You.

Give me the courage to lay down my fears at Your feet and allow You to work through my pain and insecurities. And allow my shortcomings to sing the melody of Your love as You've intended.

Time to reflect . . .

1. Whether it is a particular grief or experience, which moment in your life do you feel has been the point when you've felt at your lowest?

2. If it wasn't recently, do you feel God has used that moment or experience for His glory? If yes, how? If it was recently, how do you think He might use it if you allow Him to?

3. Raise up your heart to Him and hand Him that moment, asking Him to use it as a vessel for His love. Now write that prayer down so that you can always bring it to mind when you are struggling to let go of a hurt.

Let your faith answer the call

"Courage is resistance to fear,
Mastery of fear,
Not absence of fear."

– Mark Twain

Chapter 7

Let Your Faith Answer the Call

Courage is resistance to fear,

Mastery of fear,

Not absence of fear.

—MARK TWAIN

IT'S OKAY TO NEED A BREATHER.

It doesn't make you less.

It doesn't diminish your value.

If anything, that minute adds to your value.

It's in that minute, that moment of utter hopelessness and pure defeat, you finally see the help you need.

In that minute, you can grasp just how much you need Him to intervene, and only then are you able to surrender.

You surrender your pain.

You surrender your fears.

You surrender your will.

Because in that minute, where you sit in a silence void of all the fight that brought you here, you finally see your need for Him. You need Him to take full control, because trying to maintain control of everything and everyone has proven too big a feat.

You can't do it alone, and in that minute, you know He can.

You realize that this is your rock bottom, and it's in that minute, in your weakness, that He swoops in and proves His strength—yet again.

But He needs us to get to that minute so that we can see Him.

Amidst the chaos, the yelling, the tears, and the tantrums, we don't see Him standing there, waiting for us. He waits for us to look to Him as our source of peace and calm through the tumultuous day. But we soldier on, thinking that this is what we were meant to do. We feel that our value lies in how much we can do and solve for those who look to us for answers, but in all that doing, we lose sight of our true calling.

Yes, we're Mamas—modern heroines for the littlest and loudest people.

But above that, we are His.

We are His daughters and His love.

We are allowed to feel worn out, because in our defeat awaits a Father wanting to restore us each day so we can continue to spread His love and light.

We are allowed to feel clueless, because in our lack of answers awaits a King who sees and knows all and longs for us to call on Him.

We are allowed to take a minute, because in our pit of weakness awaits a Savior whose strength is perfected in us—while we are in that minute.

> "He said to me, 'My grace is sufficient for you, for My strength is made perfect in weakness.' Therefore most gladly I will rather boast in my infirmities, in reproaches, in needs, in persecutions in distresses, for Christ's sake. For when I am weak, then I am strong." ~ 2 Corinthians 12:9–10

It's hard asking for help.

As Mama, you might feel you need to be the problem solver, the master planner, the most prepared for any God-given natural disaster, and the one who becomes everything for everyone, no matter how fatigued and fragile it makes you. Asking for help almost feels like you're relinquishing control of those titles. Although people think you're tired of them, secretly you are grateful for the added responsibility. Somehow bearing those roles makes you feel as though you are carrying out God's work. You might feel like asking for help takes away from your value as Mama—the only role you feel you can use to bring Glory to God because He knows how badly you've messed up the other roles He's put you in.

This is your chance to show Him you're cut out for the work.

This is your chance for a do-over.

This is your chance to prove yourself worthy—once and for all.

But the role weighs heavily on you.

It takes complete control and now has you captive.

It won't let you go, even for a minute, so you can catch a breath.

Even when you try to sleep, you wake up often and frightfully, thinking about all of your shortcomings that day and all the worst-case scenarios that could declare themselves throughout the night.

In your rest, you are still Mama.

I've always struggled with asking for help. This struggle likely comes from a place of pride, but more so, I think it comes from a place of fear.

> "Now in the fourth watch of the night Jesus went to them, walking on the sea. And when His disciples saw Him walking on the sea, they were troubled, saying, 'It is a ghost!' And they cried out for fear. But immediately Jesus spoke to them, saying, 'Be of good cheer! It is I; do not be afraid.' And Peter answered Him and said, 'Lord, if it is You, command me to come to You on the water.' So He said, 'Come.' And when Peter had come down out of the boat, he walked on the water to go to Jesus. But when he saw that the wind was boisterous, he was afraid; and beginning to sink he cried out, saying, 'Lord, save me!' And immediately Jesus stretched out His hand and caught him, and said to him, 'O you of little faith, why did you doubt?'" ~ Matthew 14: 25–31

I'm only just emerging from a season of uncertainty and fear. I've stepped out of the boat, but all I have been able to see are the waves surrounding me, and all I've been able to make out ahead is the looming storm.

I haven't been able to see Him.

I haven't heard Him trying to get my attention.

Deadlines have been hanging over my head, burdens have strung my family on an anxiety-riddled road, and exhaustion only fueled the worry.

But He never left.

He walked beside me into my office and helped me write my unrealistic list of to-dos for the day ahead, even though I didn't acknowledge Him.

He whispered His presence in my ears as I wept over yet another failure, another shortcoming brought to the light for others to see, even though I didn't hear Him.

He tucked me into His embrace when I panicked about how we were going to make it to the other side of the overwhelming mountain of trials that kept defeating us, even though I couldn't feel Him.

Even though I couldn't make Him out in the middle of my fog, He was always there, and He was closer than ever, continually encouraging me to "come" and step into the chaos and uncertainty, looking only to Him.

Soon enough, it all became too much.

I remember getting to a point when everything I read or saw that reminded me of my pain brought me to tears. I was so preoccupied with my trials that I couldn't have a single conversation with anyone without excusing myself to find a place to be alone with my haunting thoughts. I reached a point when all I could hear was a ringing noise and all I could see was the thick fog created by the mist of my tears. I was so overwhelmed by everything in my life that it all came to a halt because I no longer knew how to become unstuck. The fear crippled me, and just like Peter, I was sinking.

"Lord, save me!" I cried from the pit of voiceless fear that had completely overcome me. I cried, and He heard. And even though I haven't made it above the water yet, I'm slowly coming up, hand and heart in Christ's. So I know I'll be alright.

We look to Christ, and we see His glory. We know Him through His mysteries and appreciate His power when we recognize our own limitations. Peter saw Him on the water and knew that He could do anything. He knew that if Christ called Peter to join Him on the water, he could walk alongside him.

But his limitations clouded his view of the Lord.

His weaknesses took hold of his hand when he reached for Christ.

When things got tough and the seas became unpredictable, he looked away from the source of his strength and instead could only see the uncertainty of the situation. He couldn't see beyond the physical and into the mysterious and remarkable thing that God had prepared for him. He only saw the sea.

God invites us out onto the water, into the unknown and exciting.

He waits for us to take His hand, excited for us to experience His majesty. He knows we can walk on the water with Him. All He asks is that we hold His hand and look only to Him.

The winds will rage.

The waters will swell over our feet, trying to take away our peace.

The people will look on in disbelief, trying to fill us with doubt.

But the Lord stands.

He stands waiting with his outstretched hand.

He walks forward, wanting us to see only His might.

He stills the waters so we can once again change our focus.

Though, out of His pure love, He doesn't force us into this ultimate leap of faith. He waits for us to ask to join Him on this life journey. He also doesn't expect us to have unshakable faith when we take our first step. Instead, He holds our hand while we're still learning to walk on the water and teaches us how to take our strides. When we're ready, He lets go, giving us room to bring others along.

Eventually, our faith becomes bigger than our fear.

I grew up learning that fear cannot live where faith lives.

While that might be true, it doesn't make me a failure if I can't drive out the fear with my faith.

It makes me human.

It makes me a product of the fall.

I know my God can do the impossible, and I believe with my whole heart that He loves me beyond my comprehension. But that doesn't mean I won't have days filled with anxiety over the uncertainty of this life. He knows my faith is lacking, because if it wasn't, I would be perfect. I would have finished the race. But I haven't. I'm still here. I don't think that fear and faith can't live in the same compound. I think inevitably they do—and will. But it's what I do with that fear that makes all the difference. It's how much I give it when it asks me for everything, and it's who I give that fear to when I feel most crippled by it. And that's where faith comes in.

I trust my God will take my fears—if I give them to Him—and use them in my perfection process.

I trust my God will use even the little faith I have to turn my fears into my strengths.

I trust my God, with His perfect love, will drive away my fears and fill their void with peace.

My only job is to trust Him with my fears and to keep trusting Him with them when they continue to creep into my heart.

Peter denied Jesus out of fear. Even though he knew the Lord, loved and trusted Him, he denied Him three times—only out of fear.

Even though he saw the Lord feed 5,000 men with only a basket of fish and bread, he denied Him.

Even though he saw Him walk on water, and then he himself got to walk on the water right beside Him, he denied Him.

Even though he saw Him heal the blind, heal the lame, and raise the dead, he denied Him.

Even though he knew Him as Lord and believed Him to be his Messiah, he denied him.

Only out of fear.

I don't think my faith is as strong as Peter's was, and I know my fear is far greater; yet, in that part of his life, I find the most comfort. In his denial, I can see how faith can live where there is fear. There will be moments that test our faith, and there will be moments that test our fear as well—which call we choose to answer is up to us.

Mama, we fear being alone, even though we know in our hearts how loved and surrounded we are. Most of the time, when loneliness calls, we let our insecurities and anxieties answer.

> "For He Himself has said, 'I will never leave you nor forsake you.' So we may boldly say: 'The Lord is my helper; I will not fear. What can man do to me?'" ~ Hebrews 13:5–6

Mama, we fear being wrong, even though we deeply believe that even in our failures, our Lord will bless. When indecision looms, we let our worry about things completely out of our control take over and cripple us from seeing His hand at work.

> "And we know that all things work together for good to those who love God, to those who are the called according to His purpose" ~ Romans 8:28

Mama, we fear the judgement of others for our choices, our appearance, our character, and our dearest treasures, even though we know we are daughters of the Most High and He is the only One who wants and loves us as we are. In the moment, when their piercing eyes throw daggers into our soul, we let it blind us from seeing the warmth, affirmation, and complete love that surround us every minute of every day.

> "What then shall we say to these things? If God is for us, who can be against us? He who did not spare His own Son, but delivered Him up for us all, how shall He not with Him also freely give us all things." ~ Romans 8:31–32

So I will choose faith every day. The fear will always be there, and some days, no matter how hard I try, it'll fight its way past my faith to open the door and resurface everything I try so hard to contain. But I will do my best to still choose faith, hoping that one day, the fear will have no fight left because of my faith.

Now look up!

Father,

Strengthen me so that my faith can't help but answer each of Your knocks on my heart.

I constantly allow my fear to be the governor of my days and, unfortunately, my heart. I wish to no longer be a prisoner to it, and I want faith to win the race every time. But I can't do that without Your help. Teach me how to use the fear as simply an additional force in my fight for purpose and my search for You.

Time to reflect . . .

1. What do you think you're most afraid of right now?

2. Has that fear hindered you in your relationship with God? How?

3. Write down three things you wish to say to that fear and keep them handy for whenever you feel it starting to rule.

He meets us where we are

God will meet you where you are
In order to take you where He wants
you to go.

— Tony Evans.

Chapter 8

He Meets Us Where We Are

God will meet you where you are
In order to take you where He wants you to go.

—TONY EVANS

HE SAT IN THE HEAT of the afternoon sun. Waiting.

It wouldn't be too much longer, He thought, before they finally met. Thankfully, He knew how this would go down. Still, butterflies fluttered in His stomach as He anticipated meeting His love. Although they hadn't met yet, He knew her, and He knew this was going to be a love story for the ages.

Just as His mind was wandering, picturing what their life would look like once they meet, He saw her.

Even from a distance, He could make out her brows furrowing under the pain that her wrinkles revealed. He could see her slouched shoulders burdened by the weight of her daily hurt.

He could see her.

All of her.

And He loved her.

Oh, how He longed for her love in return!

But she walked past Him and carried on with her daily grind. She had work to do, and although she tried to ignore him and avoid eye contact, her rapidly beating heart hummed so loudly that it was only a matter of time until He would hear it too. She dropped her belongings on the ground and went over to the well, as she did every day. It was a chance for her to feel valued, a daily opportunity to feel worthy. At the well, she would stand and feel the purity of the water wash away the sweat of her sins. This was her purpose. This was where she felt seen.

As she reached into the well to gather up her earnings of worth, He spoke. His words struck her with excitement and pain all at once. His voice as smooth as silk, tenderly calling out to her just as she was about to spiral into her own well of pity. Her abrasiveness didn't even deter Him; He spoke to her again. And again. He wanted her, and it seemed He wasn't taking "no" for an answer. So, she listened.

She listened as He gently reminded her of all of the hurt she had been harboring in her heart. She listened to Him lovingly explain who she really was—and what she was running from.

She listened to Him, and she loved Him.

He was the One.

The One who would bring her out of the well and into His loving arms.

The One who would restore her true purpose.

The One who loved her. As she was. Who wanted to love her forever.

I sat in silence.

I stared at the picture of Christ for what felt like forever.

But I had no words.

I don't know what exactly I was expecting to come out of this, but I sat and waited anyway. I couldn't muster anything but tears while looking into His compassionate eyes. I wanted so badly to feel His arms around me, but I hadn't felt them in so long that I feared I wouldn't remember what it felt like.

The embrace never came.

I remember asking Him where He was and why He wasn't paying any attention to me. The silence baffled me. So, I left. I felt like I was running out of tears.

I walked downstairs and immediately was met with a million mom jobs that required my attention. I wasn't in the right head-space for anything in those days, and my patience for even the least of inconveniences was wearing thin. I felt especially defeated having just left His very presence feeling invisible. Of course, my daughter was in a 'no-listening' mood, and that seems to be the one thing that always makes me lose control of my calm. I'm not a fan of time-outs, and we don't typically use them in our house, but that day, I really just needed those few minutes to think about my next action plan.

The first time-out had no effect. Nor did the second. Nor the fifth.

I was livid. I could feel my ears burning and my tongue fighting the anger it so desperately wished to yell out. I felt so defeated knowing I had not only lost control of the situation but also of myself. Nobody was listening to me—both right there in that moment and every moment I had spent on my knees beforehand.

I fell to the ground and sat with my head between my knees, feeling as though that exact moment weighed a ton and rested on my already burdened shoulders.

When I finally summoned the strength to lift my head, I saw it—the image I would carry in my subconscious to remind me of my Lord, one that would awaken my senses and allow Him to be felt again. I saw love. Pure, relentless love.

My husband quietly sat beside my daughter on the time-out step. I hadn't even noticed him step into the room; he swiftly and silently made his presence known to her. He wrapped his arms around her, and she softened with his touch. His insignificant gesture revealed a love so pure and deep that it engulfed her completely, and within minutes, there was calm.

A calm filled with sweetness.

A calm filled with warmth.

A calm only possible with self-sacrificing love.

Pure love.

Unconditional love.

They sat there for what seemed like a lifetime, talking and hashing things out. The details of the conversation weren't clear to me, but I heard the sound of her sweet voice. She could have been retelling a story or complaining about her mother. I really don't know what they spoke about on that step, but I know he met her in the place where she found herself in trouble, and he listened to her.

Oh, the taste I got of my Lord's heart that day. I throw tantrums and constantly separate myself from Him to find answers and peace. I sit on that step waiting, but the answers and peace never come. The longer I wait, the more inpatient I become. I wait for Him to bring the calm and blame Him for my isolation when the reality is that I'm the one who willingly chose the step.

But even though my choices constantly separate us, He still comes.

He always shows up.

He sits with me on that step.

With His hands on mine, He shares my hurt and confusion. The warmth from His fingertips gives my soul the embrace it desperately keeps trying to find. He joins me in my chaos, in my confusion, and in my stubbornness.

Without judgement.

Just love.

What my husband did that day truly imitated our Lord and painted the exact picture that Christian parents can strive their entire lives to create. He put his agenda and pride aside and put on love. Just love.

Just the other day, while steam might have actually been coming out of my ears as I repeated myself for what felt like the thousandth time that night, he sweetly reminded me, "We just have to love them. That's our only job." He spoke such truth in his sweetness that I was taken aback. I thought back to the last few conversations I had with my daughter and wondered how much sweetness she received from those words. Unfortunately, not much. I've told her what to do and how to do those things, and I've yelled when those things weren't done correctly. I've forced so much of me onto her without acknowledging the incredible girl standing before me. And, worst of all, I didn't show her love—unconditional, pure love.

In my husband's words, the recent few weeks flashed before me, rudely awakening the poor form I had allowed to run the show for too long. At that moment, I saw everything I was doing wrong in my parenting.

I lacked love.

Of course, I loved my daughter harder than I ever imagined possible. But the love I was showing her was the wrong kind. There were so many strings attached.

Say "yes," and you please me.

Listen to every order perfectly, and I'm in a good mood.

Show big feelings or say "no" because you had your own ideas, and I am unhappy and annoyed that you've pierced my pride.

Conditional love. That's all she knew from me.

The Samaritan woman[1] was just going about her daily tasks when our Lord met her at the well. She would even pick the middle of the day (also the hottest time of day) to do her strenuous job of filling up the heavy pitchers of water to bring back to her home so that she could avoid the scrutiny and judgment of people. She never wanted to be seen, let alone spoken to. Oh, how desperately she wanted to erase the mistakes of her past and have them washed away by the very water she drew each day. But no water would be enough to rid her of her memories. The midday sun would pierce her soul to make even the most invisible parts of the day feel like a silent interrogation. She did not know what was waiting for her at the well—the ordinary well she drew from every day.

But that day was far from ordinary.

Christ was waiting for her in that same interrogating heat. But their encounter would be anything but the interrogation she expected.

I can only imagine what she was thinking as she approached the well, seeing this strange Man sitting there, waiting for her. Was

1. The story of the Samaritan woman can be found in the gospel of John, chapter 4.

He going to scold her for her past, or make suggestions for how she should live her future? She would have been hurrying to finish what she needed to do to avoid being asked the questions she was so desperately trying to hide from.

But the Man didn't do that.

He spoke.

He spoke sweetly.

He didn't rebuke her. With love, He spoke truth and salvation to her longing soul. He showed her the love missing in her dealings with others. He met her where she was and introduced her to the love she was searching for. In her chaos and confusion, He brought the calm.

God meets us where we are, and in that place, He shows us His love.

He sits with us on that step we deliberately chose, where we sit wallowing in our hurt and confusion, and He brings peace.

The peace of knowing we are not alone here.

And the peace of knowing we are seen here.

So, Mama, rest assured that on that step of hurt, confusion, and isolation, the Lord is sitting right beside you. You might not feel the warmth of His embrace amidst your own pain, but His love will slowly etch away at the encasings holding your heart, and His mere presence will be the solace you've been searching for this entire time.

Now look up!

Father,

Help me see You right here on my lonely step. I know You are sitting beside me, waiting for me to acknowledge Your presence. But in the meantime, Lord, please fill this space with Your peace and love. Allow me to feel You there even though I might not be ready to see You.

You meet us where we are. Now just help me see You in that very place of hurt.

Time to reflect . . .

1. Think about the step you are sitting on right now. What is it, and what is keeping you there?

2. Have you been able to see God in that place of hurt? If yes, how? And if not, think about the story of the Samaritan woman and write a prayer asking God to reveal Himself to you.

Here I am Lord

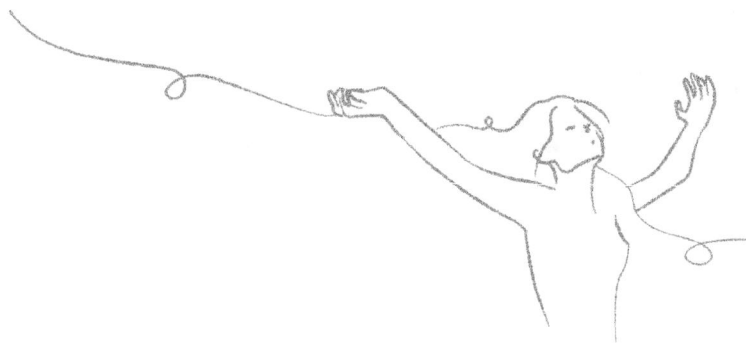

"If you want to get warm you must stand near the fire: if you want to be wet you must get into the water. If you want joy, power, peace, eternal life, you must get close to, or even into, the thing that has them. They are not a sort of prize which God could, if He chose, hand out to anyone. They are a great fountain of energy and beauty spurting up at the very centre of reality. If you are close to it, the spray will wet you: if you are not, you will remain dry. Once a man is united to God, how could he not live forever? Once a man is separated from God, what can he do but wither and die."

- C.S. Lewis, Mere Christianity

Chapter 9

Here I Am, Lord

If you want to get warm you must stand near the fire: if you want to be wet you must get into the water. If you want joy, power, peace, eternal life, you must get close to, or even into, the thing that has them. They are not a sort of prize which God could, if He chose, hand out to anyone. They are a great fountain of energy and beauty spurting up at the very center of reality. If you are close to it, the spray will wet you: if you are not, you will remain dry. Once a man is united to God, how could he not live forever? Once a man is separated from God, what can he do but wither and die.

—C.S. LEWIS, MERE CHRISTIANITY

I WAS WAITING FOR MY MIRACLE.

I was so sure it was coming.

I laid on the floor with my knees to my chest, my eyes overcome by my emotions. They had tried too hard for too long to contain the tears, but that day, their stronghold broke. I couldn't understand why. More frustrating than that, I couldn't feel Him making things better for me.

I prayed with such faith.

I cried to Him with such conviction.

"Whatever things you ask when you pray, believe that
you receive them, and you will have them." ~ Mark 11:24

Wasn't that the promise, Lord?!

I was asking in Your name and with complete and utter faith
that things would improve! Why did this promise not apply to me?!

Nothing.

No miracle.

What was I missing?

I ask that question more times than I care to admit.

Why aren't you healing that young boy?

Why aren't you supporting that single mother?

Why would you allow for such a devastating attack?

Why can't you give them a better life?

Why can't you make me whole again?

And, more recently, why did you take that precious child
away from me?

I know God has always heard my cries, and I don't doubt that
my pain moved Him. But why not intervene?

Why not intervene as I sat on the beach, holding my husband
close?

We had yet another setback, and we just sat there in silence,
holding each other, listening to the waves crash against the shore
and secretly praying for one to come wash over us, allowing us to
start anew. I had been mustering every ounce of strength I had
forged over the years to get us through the past few months, and in
that moment, it all withered away.

I needed to be there for them.

I needed them to see that I was okay, so that they could keep
fighting too.

Worse than hiding my pain from them, I was hiding my pain
from the One who could actually do something about it: God.

I was concealing my vulnerability and my hurt. I had completely stopped speaking to Him, for fear that it would all come
flooding out and I wouldn't be able to stop. Of course, I was mad,
and I expected Him to intervene even when I walked farther away

from Him. But what I was even more weary of bringing to the surface was how broken I truly was.

On that beach, I realized the injustice of my choices.

Even with my 'strength,' my husband was falling apart—and maybe it was *because of* my fraudulent facade and my commitment to concealing the very part of myself that claimed my thoughts, my emotions, my decisions, and my very personality. I had missed the effect my choices were having on everyone I hold so dear. That anxiety that I had harbored in my heart all that time was finding its way out, and although it wasn't escaping through my emotions and demeanor, it had still somehow found a route into the hearts of those I was trying to protect. I had let it govern everything about myself for so long, and I had missed just how much I was letting it rule by not bringing it to the surface and exposing it once and for all.

I was scared.

I had never let myself be so vulnerable, and I honestly didn't even know how.

Growing up, I never really spoke about what I kept concealed inside me.

I thought that by letting everything out I would be diminishing my value, that people would only see me as broken and flawed and their relationship with me would turn into one in which I was a victim. I never wanted to be seen as weak, and I wish I knew why.

Maybe it was because I had great friends at school, and I didn't want it to affect my reputation. Or because I was the eldest at home, and I felt a sense of responsibility toward my siblings, not wanting my parents to stop putting their trust in me if I let myself cry and complain about everything that hurt. Or maybe it was because I was really blessed, and there was nothing in my life that warranted complaint and I would seem ungrateful for all the gifts God was blessing me with daily. Whatever the reason, I had always kept my inner self from everyone around me.

When my husband and I began dating, this was the toughest and most challenging part of our relationship. I never opened up about things he had done that upset me. I never even opened up about my genuine desires or what I really wanted from him.

I still don't.

But I'm working on it.

I freeze up when asked to be honest about how I feel.

I hold my vulnerability so close, for fear that letting it go would mean letting go of the entire persona I created for myself over the years. I had worked too hard to just let that all dissipate with my tears. Too many tears.

Have you ever noticed what happens when you shake a soda bottle and then try to open it?

I felt like that soda bottle.

Instead of opening myself up every so often to allow others a part of me and to feel more at peace and in control, I had let every setback, every unanswered prayer, every twinge of pain, every fear, and every hurt shake me. I had ensured it all remained closed in, with the lid tightly shut, making certain that nothing was known to anyone.

But on that beach, the lid could no longer contain the rampant soda within.

The lid exploded off, and, in that moment, all my efforts seemed not only futile but harmful.

Those waves did indeed wash something away, but it wasn't what I was expecting. It forced my vulnerability to the surface and made me finally confront the person within.

In that moment, I realized what the problem was, the reason for all those months and years of deep, relentless hurt.

It was me.

I had let my pride become a hinderance to the truth.

Worst of all, I was feeding myself those lies—and believing them.

I had convinced myself for too long that I was doing okay, that I didn't need help. After all, I knew all the signs of anxiety and depression, and I was in the medical field (which, of course, meant that I was immune to its paraphernalia (yes, I'm rolling my eyes at this sentence too)). Nobody had ever really asked me if I was okay except for my mother that one time, so I was left to my own devices, and they were unfortunately convincing me I didn't need help.

But on that beach, it all became clear. My deception was not just hurting me; it was extending its stinging tentacles to those I loved most.

I wasn't okay.

I hadn't been okay for some time.

But that had to change.

On that beach, I prayed. For the first time in what felt like a lifetime, I lifted my heart to God. I said little. I just asked for help. But starting that day, I made adjustments to aid my healing. I spoke to one of my spiritual mentors and, without revealing much (old habits die hard), I managed, "I don't feel like I'm okay."

Without asking questions, he simply said, "Start by praying the Thanksgiving Prayer[1] every day, even though you might not feel thankful for much right now."

He was right. I did not feel as though I had anything to be thankful for. I felt like a fraud kneeling in front of God reciting words of thanks that I definitely did not mean. But I prayed anyway.

Initially, I could only make it through the first couple of lines.

My sadness constantly interrupted me. It would halt the words before they escaped my lips. They just sat on my heart, desperately wishing to be spoken out loud.

But it kicked off my journey of restoration.

In the months that followed, I worked hard on myself.

I wanted to get better. I needed to get better.

So, I showed up.

I showed up for my prayers.

I showed up for my Lord.

I showed up for myself.

I researched ways I could help improve my health. I spoke with other health professionals and researched evidence-based practices that could help.

---

1. The Thanksgiving Prayer is a prayer in the Agpeya prayer book, which is the Coptic Orthodox book of hours, guiding believers in their daily prayer.

I came into His presence daily. I allowed Him the time and space to work His finest work in me. I don't know what that work is, or how far along I am in the process, but daily I proclaim, "Here I am, Lord. Here, in Your presence, I'll be while You use me as You see fit."

Being present is the hardest part of the journey—showing up for yourself and for God to work His magic when everything inside you feels as though it has already given up. But because it is the hardest step, it is the most important one. As difficult as it is, while we sit with our pain, we need to silence the doubt, the hurt, and the fear and listen extra carefully for our Lord.

> "And behold, the Lord passed by, and a great and strong wind tore into the mountains and broke the rocks in pieces before the Lord, but the Lord was not in the wind; and after the wind an earthquake, but the Lord was not in the earthquake; and after the earthquake a fire, but the Lord was not in the fire; and after the fire a still small voice. So it was, when Elijah heard it, that he wrapped his face in his mantle and went out and stood in the entrance of the cave." ~ 1 Kings 19:11–13

A still, small voice.

Can you hear it?

It took me months to successfully silence the great and strong wind of doubt, the earthquake caused by my hurt, and the fire of raging fear inside me. The silencing of those elements took patience and a village—a community of family, friends, and professionals. Only when everything began working together in harmony (and with my permission) was I able to finally enjoy the stillness of my Lord.

So, Mama, close your eyes and lift your heart to He who is desperately waiting on Your attention. Stand up and declare, "Here I am, Lord," find your village, and give yourself permission to show up today—and every day.

Now look up!

Father,

I can't hear or see You yet, but I want to.

I know the first step is choosing to show up, but that is where I am stuck.

I want to stand, but my feet remain shackled by doubt. I want to see, but my hurt blinds my eyes. I want to pray, but my fear holds my heart and hands.

Lord, loosen the chains that hold me captive and give me the strength to stand up and shout, "Here I am, Lord."

Time to reflect . . .

1. What are you finding to be the hardest part of your healing journey?

2. What practical steps could you take today to break free of this painful cycle? (Think simple and achievable steps that you are ready for right now.)

3. Stand up and say, "Here I am, Lord." Attempt to begin each day with that proclamation, even though it may feel insincere.

We're all in
this together

Part of every misery is, so to speak, the misery's shadow or reflection: the fact that you don't merely suffer but have to keep on thinking about the fact that you suffer.
I not only live each endless day in grief, but live each day thinking about living each day in grief.

— A Grief Observed by C.S. Lewis

Chapter 10

We're All in This Together

Part of every misery is, so to speak, the misery's shadow or reflection:
the fact that you don't merely suffer but have to keep on thinking about
the fact that you suffer. I not only live each endless day in grief, but live
each day thinking about living each day in grief.

—C.S. LEWIS, *A GRIEF OBSERVED*

WE BRIEFLY EXPLORED THE IMPORTANCE of finding our village in
the last chapter.

> "And the Lord God said, 'It is not good that man should
> be alone; I will make him a helper comparable to him.'"
> ~ Genesis 2:18

Think of a time when you felt isolated, either physically or
emotionally. Now try to remember how your heart felt in those
moments.

God didn't create us to feel alone.

God recognized our need for companionship when He created Adam only to see just how essential it was for him to have Eve
by his side.

How much sweeter is a meal shared, a house filled with
people?

Imagine how much more bearable our pain would be as a burden shared.

We may have previously experienced the weightlessness that comes from a friend carrying a heavy load of the hurt causing our backs to ache. Yet, as I mentioned in a previous chapter, we prefer to hang on to our loads, for fear that letting even a piece of them go would mean giving up a part of who we are. We fear it'll make us less—but only less by our own flawed standards.

I only discovered the value in company after I became a mother. I found solace in seeing other people struggling with the same things I was navigating. But I only ever came to discover that others were in the same boat when I took the plunge and began talking about my own hardships. Most of us hide behind a false smile and the blatant lie that things are "fine" when asked, almost for the ease of it all, knowing that saying anything else might give birth to a long interrogation and a conversation we hoped we'd never have. What we don't consider is that those tough conversations can make way for beautiful friendships and sisterhood in our deepest pits of fear.

Imagine the joy we could find in the depth of pain when we come to find comfort in the assurance that we are not alone. We will see Christ Himself in our fiery furnace when we let His love and peace come through those around us. There is a beauty in vulnerability. But we can only find that beauty in the multiple ripples it causes and the truth that emerges from it.

On that terrible day, my husband clutched me as I sobbed.

Nothing in this life prepares you for that kind of loss—losing the child you loved but never got to meet.

All I could feel in that moment was the heat of my tears drenching even my undergarments and the strength of my husband's arms holding me, even though his inner strength couldn't quite fathom what was happening. In his hurt, he allowed my body to feel weightless while my burdened soul felt like a ton of bricks resting on my heart. I was still on the phone with my doctor at that moment, but after "I'm sorry . . . " I don't remember anything else she said.

I loved that child—I still do—and God only knows how badly I miss him (we hadn't yet found out the baby's gender, but in my heart, I truly believed that I was being gifted a boy). What followed his loss was a deep sadness, a pain that I had only ever heard of before that day—and, of course, more guilt.

Was I the reason his brief life had to end?

Was it because I continued to go for runs, or because I ate something that could have been harmful to him?

Did I not respect his home enough to allow him to thrive?

We know that around one in four women experience this hurt in their lives, but what we don't know is why.

Why the Lord would allow some losses but not others.

Why one woman will never have to endure such crushing hurt, while some feel like that is all they've ever known.

In a matter of seconds, the pain of this entire community was mine too. It definitely wasn't a club I wanted to be part of, but it was a club.

I wasn't alone.

Knowing my mom was in this club was a weird comfort for me.

She didn't tell me to "thank God, because it could have been worse."

She didn't tell me to "cheer up, because others have it harder."

She just listened to the story my tears were telling her through the phone speaker and continued to reassure me that this wasn't my fault. She repeated those few words many times, hoping they would eventually stick. She needed me to believe her. And as hard as that was for me, eventually I did.

No lectures.

No advice.

No words of wisdom.

Just pure love—the enemy of self-pity. But it felt like a lifetime before the self-pity was truly defeated.

Everything seemed to fade to black the day I had my surgery for my miscarriage. The finality of that moment hit me harder than anything I've ever experienced. I remember opening my eyes and feeling an indescribable pain. The nurse noticed me trying to mouth the word "pain" through the emotions that were silencing my voice and immediately rushed to give me something. The pain vanished almost instantly, and it took with it my ability to conceal my feelings.

I cried. I felt as though I would never stop.

The nurse knew exactly what to do at that moment. I wish I remembered his name, or even what he looked like, but all I can recall is my sorrow. He swiftly moved my bed to a private room—probably reserved for an infectious patient and not a hysterical one—and handed me over to another two nurses who, without speaking, looked after my heart and body. One closed the door while the other came over to hug me, all the while whispering affirmations and loving-kindness in my ear. She held me close and spoke to me about her own daughter's hurt, having recently been through the same thing.

She, too, was experiencing a pain so deep, so piercing.

She, too, was a part of this dreaded club.

During that period, I turned to one other friend who understood this loss. She cried with me and gave me the space and permission I needed to edge closer to healing through her own pain and journey. She welcomed me into the club with nothing but love. Pure love.

But sadly, that was not the only response I got during that time. I was sitting across from someone having lunch when they asked, "Why are you sad all the time?" They knew exactly what I was going through; yet, they still asked. I felt as though they had just pierced a dagger into my heart and then blamed me for allowing it to hurt me. They believed I had full control over my grief.

Grief never actually leaves. It lingers around forever, but it isn't always vocal.

It speaks and stays silent.

It yells and timidly shies away.

It brings you to your knees and gives you the strength to stand tall.

But when it speaks, it demands to be heard.

When it yells, it holds your attention captive.

When it brings you to your knees, it forces memory, even when all you want to do is forget.

Although grief has a way of robbing us of the joy we feel in a moment and instilling us with guilt when we begin to believe again, it also reminds us of what we have and who we are. We are emotional beings, beings able to feel everything that makes us and breaks us. Grief allows us to connect to everyone and everything in this life, including our Lord Himself.

> "And He was withdrawn from them about a stone's throw, and He knelt down and prayed, saying, 'Father, if it is Your will, take this cup away from Me; nevertheless not My will, but Yours, be done.' Then an angel appeared to Him from heaven, strengthening Him. And being in agony, He prayed more earnestly. Then His sweat became like great drops of blood falling down to the ground." ~ Luke 22:41–44

Our grief unites us with our Lord's moment of agony in the garden before His crucifixion, a grief so loud it made His body bleed.

Now picture your own pain, your own loss, the reason for your grief.

Remember its pangs.

Remember the moments of joy it has stolen.

Remember its deafening silence in your isolation.

Now, read the above scriptural account again.

Read about our Lord's prayer and pleadings. Read about the honesty in His agony. And although He was only a "stone's throw" from the others, read about His isolation. The grief gripped Him, mind and body.

Grief blinds us to the truth of our worth and separates us from the love that surrounds us. But in grief, we are never alone. It is the invisible string that envelops each of us into the warm embrace of our Lord, who Himself has felt our hurt and lived through our pain.

I knew my Lord was right there amidst my pain. Just as He never put out the fire for the three young men in the book of Daniel[1] but joined them in its heat, protecting them from its stings, I believed He was standing right there with me. He was not removing my sadness but sharing my hurt and crying pained tears alongside me. Even though those months after loss became a renewal for my heart and mind, I trusted that was the gift God had allowed because He felt how deeply this blow wounded me. It was His way of protecting me from the heat of my furnace. It definitely didn't seem like that was the case in the actual heart of the flame, but it was something that I discovered during my growth.

The pain of losing someone you love, along with a myriad of investigations to rule out a cancer scare—it feels truly surreal writing those words down—has a way of making you check out of the 'real world.' All I remember thinking when my doctor told me he was trying to rule out cancer was, "This must be some kind of joke." The news didn't shake me as much as it did my family.

They fasted, attended liturgies, and prayed. A lot.

They needed God to intervene and make things better.

But I felt numb. I couldn't feel their same fervency in my prayer.

After everything I had gone through—the pain of loss, allowing grief to make my heart its permanent residence, hurting for so long, only to have the small progress of healing ripped out from underneath my weary feet—I felt nothing. How could I? I had cried so many tears that my eyes felt dry. I mean, how long can someone bleed from an already severed limb? Or extract water from a dry well? It wasn't possible . . .

But even in the depths of what almost felt like despair, I had hope. I hoped that since God allowed me to see the sunshine after my year in darkness, even if it was just a glimpse, it was still there. I just couldn't see it right now. It felt like this added layer of hurt was just patching up the small window of visibility I had into the hope I had found. It wanted so badly to take that glimmer away

1. Read the book of Daniel chapter 3 for the full story.

from me. But I knew that hope was still there; it was just being concealed by the hurt.

I was numb, yes. But I was hopeful.

To me, this was nothing more than an extra chapter in my life's story. I didn't know how this one would end, but I knew it was making way for the next one—and the next one was going to be good.

I don't know what season of life you're in at this moment, but I know some seasons are hard—really hard. And the difficult moments, although we may feel like the pain will hold us victim forever, pass. They pass and their memory is replaced by beauty in the pain and wisdom in perspective.

So, Mama, hold on. This moment will indeed pass. But before it vanishes, close your eyes and savor the pain. What is the value in this pain, and what is it trying to teach you? Don't get me wrong, nothing can inject sweetness into a season of confusion and deep hurt. But God can allow for sweetness to emerge from its embers. The fire grows rampant when you're in it, but once it is extinguished, the soil recovers and from it grows the most beautiful garden, filled with new and exciting opportunities.

The fire will end.

When, I don't know.

But it will end.

Remember its pain and carry it with you. Don't let it rule you, but give it space in your heart forever so that the flowers that flourish in its wreckage smell all the sweeter.

Now look up!

Father,

In my burning furnace, I can't see Your face. But I know You are right there with me, I just can't make out Your compassionate eyes and Your reassuring smile. I know this fire will eventually be quenched by its own limitations, but while it tears through everything I love, I can't help but be overcome by its pangs.

Clear the smoke so that I can see glimpses of You. Allow those glimpses to be the glimmers of hope I need to get me to the garden of flowers I'm desperately waiting for.

Time to reflect . . .

1. If you're in the middle of your fire, what is the worst thing about this moment? If you feel you are finally emerging from a difficult season, try to think of one thing you are thankful for now that it has passed.

2. Think about your village. Who are the people in your life you feel closest to and what things have brought you together?

3. Now go back to that difficult season and write about the pain you felt and something you're thankful for because of it. Keep that piece of paper handy because we will need to learn how to embrace pain moving forward.

Mama, it's time to come forth

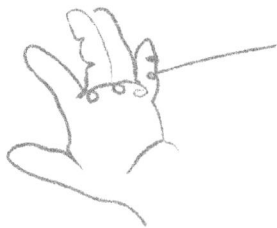

Come and see yourself through
His gracious and forgiving eyes.
Because I promise you, that if
you can do that, you will see the
strength, beauty, joy, fervour,
purity, resilience, grace, and
perfection that He sees when He
looks at you.
He loves you.
Now you need to love you.

Chapter 11

Mama, It's Time to Come Forth

Come and see yourself through His gracious and forgiving eyes. Because I promise you that if you can do that, you will see the strength, beauty, joy, fervor, purity, resilience, grace, and perfection that He sees when He looks at you. He loves you. Now you need to love you.

—MIRETTE ABRAHAM

SOMETIMES I WANT A SNAPSHOT OF A MOMENT.

But not for the reasons you might think.

Everybody says that time moves so fast that every moment is fleeting in this story of life. They say to savor the sleepless nights, the sniffly cuddles, the tantrums, the incessant interrogations, the cute rebellion, and everything that makes creating little personalities possible.

But what if you can't enjoy them?

What if you are so worn and torn that these experiences continue to prove just how numb and cold you've become?

You can't enjoy them. They only serve as a constant reminder of how exhausted you are, continuing to wear you down.

You want to take a snapshot because you fear things will get worse and you will become a different version of yourself yet again. You don't know who you'll be when the next trial comes along, and you want to remember who you are in that very moment, because you can't remember the 'you' that was, and inevitably, when things continue to poke through you, you won't remember the 'you' that is right now.

But you can't.

Instead, you continue to spiral.

She's not the reason I'm in this fog, but because of this fog, she continues to lose me. I don't know what she sees when she looks at me, and similarly, I don't know what she'll remember about this time. But I hope she learns that through the entire journey, she was my only rainbow, the only light I could see through the seemingly never-ending darkness. She was the reason I pursued healing, and she continues to be my inspiration. I want to be her reason for something greater one day.

> I pray she sees the love I continued to pour on her from my negative supply.
> I pray she remembers all the cuddles we shared and not the lack of warmth in them.
> I pray she remembers all the acts of service that she was a part of and not that they were a feeble attempt at trying to find my Lord again.
> I pray she remembers all the prayers that we prayed together and not the place of pain that they came from.
> I pray she remembers my smiles and not my sadness.
> I pray she remembers my laughter and not my tears.
> I pray she remembers my joy and not my frustrations and outbursts.
> I pray she thinks of me in love and not with hurt.

"Are you happy with me, mom?"

Her question stopped my spiraling thoughts dead in their tracks. My three-year-old asking me such a profound question, asking if my sorrow and palpable hurt was because of her. Oh, how my heart broke at that moment! It shattered with the knowledge of what my daughter thought of herself because of my lack of presence.

In my darkness, I was completely oblivious to the infectious hurt spreading. I sat and watched it slowly spread and inject the same doubt, hurt, and fears it had successfully filled my heart and mind with over the past few years into those of my closest loves.

The worst part was that I let it.

I had lost all control of its venom, and now I had lost my strength to fight.

In that moment, her words filled me with sadness, knowing that by ignoring the darkness and not paying it the respect it demanded, I had failed her as a mother. Again, I was reminded of the injustice in my choices. But this time, I had fallen deeper in the pit, and getting out would not be easy.

I wrapped her in my arms and cried, kissing her forehead repeatedly.

I wished that moment had never happened because of the slap in the face it delivered. But it ultimately woke me up from a deep sleep of denial I thought I was enjoying.

I needed to take back control.

I had made so many small steps, but at that point, something drastic had to happen.

But how?

How was I going to leave the comfort of my tomb?

The story of Lazarus is one of my favorite moments recorded of Christ's life in the Gospels. So many parts of the story continue to resonate powerfully with me, and it's in the moment of his death that we get a true glimpse of our Lord's heart.

If you're familiar with the story, you'll know that Christ didn't go to Lazarus as soon as He found out he was unwell. Instead, "He stayed two more days in the place where He was" (John 11:6). Even more confusing, the verse directly before that one specifically makes note that "Jesus loved Martha and her sister and Lazarus" (John 11:5) and continues as though to say that because of His love, He didn't go right away.

Lord, because of Your love for them, You let him die?

Is that what John is trying to say?

Mary and Martha would have felt the most alone in Lazarus' death. They were the ones who asked Him to come and bring healing, but He didn't. Mary was the one who anointed "the Lord with fragrant oil and wiped His feet with her hair" (John 11:2), but that wasn't enough to bring Him when they called.

Yet their faith in Him never wavered.

They waited on their Lord, certain that He would come in the nick of time and heal His friend before he died.

But He didn't come.

And Lazarus died.

Not only had he already died, but by the time Jesus finally got to him, he had been dead for four days! Death had not only claimed its victory, but its stench had decayed what was left of him.

Imagine the agony Lazarus had to endure sitting and waiting for death.

Like Lazarus, I sat in my tomb and waited for Christ to come.

I sat in that darkness, wallowing in my sadness and trying so hard to embrace my pain. But the longer I sat in that empty void, the louder the pain became.

Isolating silence doesn't leave much room for the person victim to its hollows to embrace anything other than its darkness. And darkness doesn't let you embrace the pain. It just heightens its pitches and stresses its stings.

Embracing pain doesn't mean cornering it into an isolated corner and giving it reign to further interrogate you.

Because in that darkness—in your loneliness—it thrives.

It surrounds you with its pangs and ensures you can't find a way out of its grip.

Where it fails is in the light, surrounded by love and company.

Christ allowed Lazarus to die.

He allowed him to be swallowed by pain and concede defeat.

We read that story, and we know, along with everyone else who stood witness, that if Christ had only gotten there sooner like they had asked, Lazarus would not have died. He would not have had to endure the pangs of pain that preceded his departure. Instead, he would have been healed, and he would have never had to enter the darkness and isolation that awaited him in that tomb.

Christ knew that too.

When He got to the tomb, "Jesus wept" (John 11:35). He loved him, and He grieved the loss of His friend. He grieved the pain that he had to endure without Him being there for him. He grieved the isolation that he felt and the uncertainty that beheld him without his friend Jesus there.

But unlike the rest of us, Jesus knew why He had to wait.

He knew why Lazarus had to die and why He couldn't merely save him from illness.

He knew He needed to save him from more than physical death.

He needed to save him from eternal death.

"Lazarus, come forth!" (John 11:43).

Imagine everyone's shock as Lazarus, wrapped in his grave-clothes, came out of that tomb—walking!

Everyone expects healing at our Lord's command. But nobody expects to be raised from the dead.

But notice how Christ still made Lazarus walk himself out of that tomb.

I imagine being raised from the dead feels a lot harder than being awoken from a deep sleep. I imagine when Lazarus heard his name being called, his body felt as though it might fail him if he tried to stand up. Pain had *overcome* Lazarus, and his life succumbed to its strength. And now, Christ was asking him to move his very fatigued body, exit the darkness that had become his resting place, and step into the bright light that would surely burn his retinas and expose his battle scars for the world to see.

How enticing would it have been for Lazarus to remain in that darkness?

After all, he had already tasted death—the worst thing that pain could throw at him. It would have been almost understandable if he had decided to just lay there, in that darkness, and remain in his state of surrender.

But he didn't.

He heard the call, and he answered it.

Jesus needed him to walk out of that tomb. To make the choice to make such a dramatic change. To willingly choose the light. To expose the hurt that had been keeping him in that tomb.

Light beautifully breaks the grip of pain, and love allows you to be the one doing the interrogating.

Outside of that tomb, pain no longer has the upper hand.

Instead, it surrenders, falls on its knees, and finally sets up camp in your heart. And only once our hearts contain it can we truly learn to embrace its presence and allow it to become a part of who we are rather than merely playing victim to its crimes.

I don't know who you are or where you're heading, but I know that you're loved.

You are loved more than you can even comprehend, and He is with you every step of the way, no matter how alone you feel.

You feel alone in your pain, and you feel unseen in your moment.

But He feels and sees you.

Your pain is His hurt.

Your sorrow is His burden.

In this moment, He is waiting outside your dark tomb, calling out for you to untangle yourself from the linen that is trying to keep you trapped in your guilt, sadness, and fear. He has resurrected you from your past life and is waiting for you to take those life-giving steps toward Him into His light.

I know it's hard to walk out of the darkness when it's all you've known for so long. I know you can't imagine anything more than the pain that has held you close and the clouds that have filled your mind, and it's terrifying not knowing what awaits you. You've known the darkness for a while, and it has become so predictable that anything other than its noise seems daunting and unknown.

But just close your eyes for a minute and listen.

Can you hear the Lord's voice?

Can you make out His whispered words of admiration?

If you can't hear Him, unwrap the linen around your ears and try again.

Still nothing?

Slowly start freeing your eyes and look for His light.

Start searching for the grace that abounds and the hope that awaits you on the other side of that tombstone.

Call out to Him and ask for directions.

Ask Him to show you the way out.

Because He knows. And more than anything, He wants you to join Him.

So, Mama, pick yourself out of, well . . . you. Come and find your true self in the One who holds you in His heart and hands. Come and see yourself through His gracious and forgiving eyes.

Because I promise that if you can do that, you will see the strength, beauty, joy, fervor, purity, resilience, grace, and perfection that He sees when He looks at you.

He loves you.

Now you need to love you.

Now look up!

Father,

Call me out of this darkness.

I'm ready to come out, but I don't know how. Sometimes I can hear Your soft callings for me from outside my tomb, but my pain is loud in here.

Help me find a way out of here and make my way toward Your tender and loving voice.

I want to feel the light on my skin again, but I know I won't make it outside without You.

Help me see myself through Your eyes so that I can see how truly loved I am. Allow that knowledge to be the strength I need to stand up and do whatever necessary to reach You.

Time to reflect . . .

1. Write three truths about yourself from God's perspective.

2. Find a Bible passage/verse to back up each of those truths. Write them down.

3. Bring out the piece of paper about your pain that you kept from the last chapter. Keep that one and the one you're writing right now together. Whenever you feel the pain hindering your progress, read the affirmations and remind yourself of who you are and how strong you truly are in the embrace of your perfect Love. He wants you as you are and wants to love you ferociously, no matter how broken you feel right now. Let that piece of paper affirm who you are in front of your pain, and let your pain be reminded that love is in control.

4. Write a list of other practical actions you can take whenever you feel the pain taking over. They can include things like journaling, speaking to someone (friend or professional), prayer, crafting, or whatever you feel you need in that moment.

Conclusion

If you're going to live, leave a legacy. Make a mark on the world that
can't be erased.

—MAYA ANGELOU

AFTER MY MISCARRIAGE, I couldn't believe that things were getting worse even though I was making the conscious choice to walk
toward the light. I felt as though I walked that road alone, but I
kept silent and continued to listen for my Lord's voice calling me
outside. I refused to return to that bed I had been laying on in the
darkness for so long, where the pitch-black ambiance had become
a suffocating presence.

So, I kept walking.

I kept venturing further into uncertainty that would soon
become hope.

One night, soon after my miscarriage surgery, I was kneeling
with my daughter as she was saying her nighttime prayers. If you're
a parent who dreads bedtimes, you know that prayer time is the
one moment when peace ensues and you can hear your rampant
thoughts again. I was deep in my thoughts when her prayer sent a
jolt down my spine, followed by such a deep sadness that I couldn't
stop the tears from running down my cheeks.

"Please God, give me a baby sister."

I couldn't believe it.

So soon after I had lost a child, this was her prayer?!

She did not know what we had all just been through, so there's no way that was the reason for her prayer.

What could have possibly led her to pray for something so personal and so specific? She had never asked for siblings, or even mentioned them, before that night.

That became her prayer every single night.

Each night, she stood before God and asked for a baby sister. And each night, my heart ached.

But, after a few short months, God heard her prayer.

Her baby sister was on her way, and she was due to arrive on her birthday!

I want my life to tell a story. I want my life to harmonize with my Lord's song He has written for me. I want to feel as though I am part of something bigger, something that'll change the world.

But I get caught up in the little details that add nothing to the finished product—and often contribute to my constant stalling and shame.

I focus on how my friends have been living out their story.

I look for inspiration on social media, a place that only stirs up more anxiety around my insecurities.

I search beside me and try so hard to make someone else's story my own, forcing my jagged-edged puzzle pieces into spaces that so obviously can't accommodate me.

I become so obsessed with the picture that my life is painting, rather than the narrative it wants to create.

Although my narrative so far has indeed been filled with much sadness and confusion, God has continued to show His hand even when I can't see it.

I'm still learning how to give pain residence in my heart and allow it to become a part of who I am—not the ruler of me, although honestly sometimes it seems easier to just let it run the show. Some days it forces me to the ground and deafens my senses to anything else that is real, and on those days, I just want to let it have its way. Then I beat myself up for letting it win. I feel like a failure, and again, feelings of worthlessness creep up.

But I need to remind myself that embracing pain is a perpetual work.

Learning to live with pain—not despite it—takes an entire lifetime.

Some days the pain needs to be heard and, in order for us to pay attention, everything else is still. Other days it seems easier to move past its cries. All the days deserve their space. And I need all the days for pain's ultimate embrace.

All we need on this journey is some grace.

And God is right there reminding us of the grace that awaits us in His arms.

We just need to listen for His call and keep walking toward Him.

Remember, sometimes, of no fault of our own, our pain can rewire our faculties and the help we need goes beyond all the things listed in this book. If you feel as though you might need that extra help, go find it! Nobody will force you to. Show up for yourself by finding that help when you need it. You won't regret taking that step. You will be glad you loved yourself enough, like Christ loves you, to tend to your heart and mind. Grab the grace that awaits you in His embrace and allow it to propel you in the direction you need to go.

God holds our pain so close while He eagerly expects our return to Him.

He tends to it while He continues to call us ever so gently, encouraging us to learn how to embrace it in His presence.

Because that's the key.

His presence.

His presence becomes the key to embracing our pain. In His presence we learn how to break free from its stronghold and tend to it as God has been doing all of these years.

He cares, Mama. He really cares.

And His care teaches us how to truly live hopefully in the trenches of our motherhood.

Further Reading

Risen Motherhood: Gospel Hope for Everyday Moments
By: Emily Jensen and Laura Wifler

Every Bitter Thing Is Sweet: Tasting the Goodness of God in All Things
By: Sarah Hagerty

Truth Unchanging: Hearing God Daily in the Midst of Motherhood
By: Becky Thompson

Try Softer: A Fresh Approach to Move Us out of Anxiety, Stress, and Survival Mode—and into a Life of Connection and Joy
By: Aundi Kolber

Get Out of Your Head: Stopping the Spiral of Toxic Thoughts
By: Jennie Allen

It's Okay Not to Be Okay: Moving Forward One Day at a Time
By: Sheila Walsh

Living on Purpose, for a Purpose
By: Joyce Meyer

Undaunted: Daring to Do What God Calls You to Do
By: Christine Caine
Foreword by: Max Lucado

About the Author

Mirette Abraham is a mother and medical doctor living and working in Sydney, Australia. After high school, she went on to complete a Bachelor of Medical Studies and Medical Doctor degree and has been employed as a full-time doctor ever since. Mirette is currently working in cancer care, dealing with patients who have a diagnosis of cancer and those in the terminal stages of their life. She is a girl mom with one four-year-old girl and another girl on the way! Mirette also serves at her local church as a Sunday School teacher, youth leader, and motivational speaker, and she is featured as a speaker and a singer on the Upper Room Media application. She has her own podcast—called *MAMI*—that speaks to the modern Orthodox mama, on which Mirette and her co-host try to work through a lot of the common struggles of motherhood in faith.

www.ingramcontent.com/pod-product-compliance
Lightning Source LLC
Chambersburg PA
CBHW070453090426
42735CB00012B/2530